UNDER

THE

NAKBA

TREE

OUR LIVES: DIARY, MEMOIR, AND LETTERS

Social history contests the construction of the past as the story of elites—a grand narrative dedicated to the actions of those in power. Our Lives seeks instead to make available voices from the past that might otherwise remain unheard. By foregrounding the experience of ordinary individuals, the series aims to demonstrate that history is ultimately the story of our lives, lives constituted in part by our response to the issues and events of the era into which we are born. Many of the voices in the series thus speak in the context of political and social events of the sort about which historians have traditionally written. What they have to say fills in the details, creating a richly varied portrait that celebrates the concrete, allowing broader historical settings to emerge between the lines. The series invites materials that are engagingly written and that contribute in some way to our understanding of the relationship between the individual and the collective. Manuscripts that include an introduction or epilogue that contextualizes the primary materials and reflects on their significance will be preferred.

MOWAFA SAID HOUSEH

Under the Nakba Tree

FRAGMENTS OF A
PALESTINIAN FAMILY
IN CANADA

◊ AU PRESS

Copyright © 2022 Mowafa Said Househ
Published by AU Press, Athabasca University
1 University Drive, Athabasca, AB T9S 3A3
https://doi.org/10.15215/aupress/9781771992039.01

Cover and interior design by Natalie Olsen, kisscutdesign.com
Cover image: Shadow Trees by Marcel / Stocksy.com
Printed and bound in Canada

Library and Archives Canada Cataloguing in Publication
Title: Under the nakba tree : fragments of a Palestinian family in Canada
/ Mowafa Said Househ.
Names: Househ, Mowafa Said, 1977–, author.
Series: Our lives (Edmonton, Alta.)
Description: Series statement: Our lives: diary, memoir, and letters
Identifiers: Canadiana (print) 20189051019 | Canadiana (ebook) 20189051027
| ISBN 9781771992039 (softcover) | ISBN 9781771992046 (PDF) | ISBN
9781771992053 (EPUB) | ISBN 9781771992060 (Kindle)
Subjects: LCSH: Househ, Mowafa Said, 1977– | LCSH: Househ, Mowafa
Said, 1977– —Family. | LCSH: Refugees—Palestine—Biography. | LCSH:
Refugees—Canada—Biography. | LCSH: Refugees, Palestinian Arab—
Canada—Biography. | LCSH: Intergenerational relations. | LCSH: Psychic
trauma. | LCSH: Canada—Ethnic relations. | CSH: Palestinian Canadians—
Biography. | LCGFT: Autobiographies.
Classification: LCC FC106.P35 H68 2022 | DDC 971/.00492740092—DC23

We acknowledge the financial support of the Government of Canada
through the Canada Book Fund (CBF) for our publishing activities and the
assistance provided by the Government of Alberta through the Alberta
Media Fund.

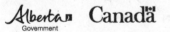

For my people and their struggle for freedom

CONTENTS

Exile is strangely compelling to think about but terrible to experience. It is the unhealable rift forced between a human being and a native place, between the self and its true home: its essential sadness can never be surmounted. And while it is true that literature and history contain heroic, romantic, glorious, even triumphant episodes in an exile's life, these are no more than efforts meant to overcome the crippling sorrow of estrangement. The achievements of exile are permanently undermined by the loss of something left behind forever.

EDWARD SAID

Reflections on Exile

1

Fleeing and Frozen

"We really would like to thank you for all this hospitality and the warm welcome and all the staff—we felt ourselves at home and we felt ourselves highly respected," Kevork Jamkossian, one of the first Syrian refugees to arrive in Canada on 11 December 2015, told Prime Minister Justin Trudeau.

"Welcome home," the new prime minister replied.

It was not always like that. Not for everybody. For Palestinians, "home" is a complicated term, and hospitality is not the first Canadian character trait I think of when I try to describe my experience of growing up Muslim in Canada.

Snow was falling in southwest Calgary as the afternoon light began to fade that December evening in 2013. Soon it would time for the *maghrib* prayer. My father and I were sitting at my brother's kitchen table, snacking on a bowl of chips and chatting before dinner. I looked over at my father.

"Yaba, remember when you made me stand outside Al-Rashid Mosque with a gun?"

"Yes, of course. I don't think I will ever forget that time." He spoke in Arabic, as he always has to his children. It was his small way of protecting his heritage and his new home in his adopted country, Canada. "Of course I remember. I said, 'Here is your weapon.'"

I, too, remember that day. My father had handed me an unloaded twenty-dollar pellet gun and left me at the doors of Al-Rashid Mosque, the oldest mosque in his new country. There I stood on a December evening in 1990, a frightened thirteen-year-old Palestinian boy holding a gun in this welcoming home the prime minister and Kevork Jamkossian had spoken about. I paced in and out of the double doors. Trying to stay visible. Trying to stay warm. I should not have been there at all. I was a teenager trying to discover how I fit into this world, a child who suddenly found himself thrown into an adult world. I still had to learn that adulthood comes early in Palestine, and that my teenage fears were trivial by comparison to what I witnessed when I visited Palestine a few years later. But that night, this terrifying and violent world was still new to me. I was not afraid of someone attacking the mosque as much as I was worried that people might question me and that I would not know how to respond, or that the police might find the gun. I felt confused but ready to defend my community at all costs.

As my father and I chatted, it struck me that more than two decades had passed since the First Persian Gulf War of 1990–91, when the chaos George W. Bush unleashed with the American invasion of Iraq became the pretext under which Canadians had joined an international coalition to defeat Saddam Hussein after Iraq had invaded neighbouring Kuwait. It was the first time Canadian troops had seen active duty in many years, and many people were proud to be part of this international coalition. As a child at the time of the Gulf War, I did not understand all the nuances the adults were discussing, but with the unerring acumen of youth, I understood what mattered and felt the ramifications to my core: Saddam was Muslim and an Arab. I was

Muslim and an Arab. In the minds of other teenagers at school, that made me the target. In this battle between the United States of America and Saddam Hussein, I became the enemy, and there was no place for me and my family in these self-involved displays of Canadian patriotic spirit.

Islam and living our faith were important to my mother when we were children, and it still is. She taught us how to pray and memorize parts of the Qur'an. When we moved to Jordan for a few years, my family lived conservatively and devoutly. When we moved backed to Canada in 1988 and I started Grade 6, I felt the culture shock and struggled to fit in. I continued to pray but did so less and less often. By Grade 8 I had stopped praying altogether because it wasn't cool. No one among my friends at school prayed except when they were at the mosque, and I did not want to be the odd one out among them when I already felt ostracized from other communities in Edmonton. Slowly, I grew apart from my faith, but I continued to lie to my mother when she asked about my faith, telling her that I prayed regularly. Perhaps my own alienation from my faith and my culture, and my desire to fit into the broader community in Edmonton, contributed to my shock at how badly Muslims were treated when the Gulf War broke out in 1990. The only way I knew how to respond to the hatred I saw and felt was to emphasize who I am, a Palestinian Muslim. My embrace of this identity was also inspired by Yazan Haymour, the president of the Canadian Arab Friendship Association, who taught us to be proud of being Arab and to acknowledge our many achievements throughout history. And so began a slow and troubled journey back to my faith and into my sense of being Arab in this world.

Although my father believed in God, he was not especially religious. But he was angry. For my father, meeting at the mosque with other families was the thing to do for the community at the time. So the mosque became part of our lives. The imam of our mosque had spoken out in opposition to Canada's participation in the war, and now the mosque—a symbol of our struggle to arrive, worship, and belong in this self-proudly multicultural country—had been vandalized. Spray paint trickled ominously down the pristine white walls, and everyone wondered whether the mosque would be the target of further attacks. No one had called on the community to defend the mosque, yet I was pressed into duty. My father had never been politically minded and did not get involved in politics all that often, but he did support the struggle for the liberation of Palestine. This war affected him and people he knew personally, and the only way he knew to show his support and to feel like he was doing something to assist his people in a time of need was to make me stand out in the cold and dark with an unloaded Canadian Tire pellet gun. And he expected me not to snivel, get angry, or beg to go home.

Home. It is a word that haunts me. My father was six months old when the Israeli Defense Forces swept into Lydda, Palestine, in July 1948. As the *New Yorker* reported in October 2013, Yitzak Rabin, the deputy commander of Operation Danny (the code name for the capture of Ramle and Lydda), gave clear instructions: "The inhabitants of Lydda must be expelled quickly, without regard to age." Lydda. My father's home. The home of his parents and his grandparents. The home that he would never know. As the IDF swept into town, some residents remained. Others fled. My grandfather Mahmoud, my grandma Nima, and eight of their nine children were among those who fled to the Arab front lines. One son, Darwish, chose to stay and fight and rejoined the family later. My grandparents had heard that the Arab Legion was waiting at the end of the road in Barfiliya to provide shelter and supplies to the people who made it there. But one hot summer night along the way, facing exhaustion, thirst, hunger, and uncertainty, my grandmother had a terrible decision to make. She was a large woman, and strong, but this was too much for her. Hoping someone else would find him and care for him, she wrapped her baby son in a blanket and left him under a tree.

Ten long minutes later, she panicked. She sent two of her other sons, Faisal and Saleh, back to get the infant—screaming at them, gasping that they must go. Now. Quickly. The baby was soon back in her aching arms, his dark eyes looking up at her. She held him close, and the journey continued.

My father would grow up in the El-Hussein refugee camp in Amman, Jordan, where he eventually became a pharmacy assistant and used his knowledge of medicines to serve people from the camp. As an adult, he would trade the hills of Jordan and Palestine for the plains of Alberta, Canada. In Alberta, thousands of miles away from the places of his birth and childhood, he would become part of another displaced Arab Muslim community. It was a place where his Jordanian pharmaceutical diploma was of no use. His pharmacist's hands became worn and tough in a cement factory; then he worked as a travelling salesman. As an immigrant to a country founded on displacement, my father again became a success at serving people.

All families have their standard jokes and stories that help them stick together even in the face of adversity. According to one of our family stories, when my grandmother sent Faisal and Saleh back to rescue the infant she had abandoned, they accidentally picked up the wrong child. To this day, if my dad's behaviour seems erratic or his character flawed—like when someone asks why he isn't as devout as the rest of his family—someone is bound to tell that story.

Now, in 2013, my father and I were sitting at the kitchen table in Calgary. I had come from Saudi Arabia, where I was working at that time, to be at this family reunion, along with my wife, who was expecting our third child, and our two daughters. I gazed out the frosted window of my brother's home and watched my children playing with their cousins in the snow. I thought of the children growing up under Israeli occupation. My Canadian nieces and nephews might be called "little terrorists" by angry whites, but they were relatively secure. They did not have to grow up too soon, like so many Palestinian children in the occupied territories of East Jerusalem, the Gaza Strip, and the West Bank, where lethal encounters are as commonplace as walking to school. Their parents did not have to sneak out at night to try to find food, running and hiding, risking being shot or captured, while their families waited locked inside their homes, praying for them to come back alive.

Dinner was a time when everyone could get together and share stories. My father and I tucked into the feast before us, tearing off pieces of flatbread—the tastiest way to scoop up a piece of kabab and a dollop of hummus—while we listened to the conversations and stories happening around the table. Across the array of aromatic dishes, recipes passed down among family members along with the stories of our survival, I looked at my father and uncles who had grown up in a camp. *Not much meat to scoop up there,* I thought. *With that body memory of hunger, how do they experience eating now?*

At times in our family history, food—real food—was only a distant memory. That hunger, not only for nourishment but also for some measure of stability, has never left my father. Anyone who goes to his place for dinner must stay until they have gained ten pounds, and he will weigh them. Well, that's an exaggeration, but I can feel how he is trying to compensate for previous imbalances by piling the food onto your plate. My brothers and sister and I have asked him about his difficult childhood. Tears well up in his eyes as he tells us, "I wish I could have been a better father, but I grew up in a camp and didn't know any better."

I have an old photo of myself with him on the couch. Over the course of many moves around the world, the photo has been buried in a box I can't find, but I only need to close my eyes to see it: In the photo, I'm sporting a young man's beard and I have my arm around him. But the composition of the photo looks forced—he is sitting in the corner, not smiling, shrinking away even as my arm extends to link us. After enduring as much hardship as he had while growing up, it was difficult for him to express things. All the same, he had agreed to let me record his stories during this visit, and I sat listening to him.

Some stories I had already heard, and, as he shared more, I realized that my father was not alone in these stories. They were the stories of my family. They were Palestinian stories—stories of displacement, separation, and sacrifice, and of solidarity and survival.

2

Calls to Prayer

My name is Mowafa Said Househ. This is not the whole truth. My name in Arabic is Mowafaq. In English it sounds like "Mowa-fuck." I did not change my name legally, but in Grade 8, I dropped the last letter to stop the endless bullying, and no one asked. In the Levant dialect of Arabic, the dialect my mother speaks, the *q* is silent. To her I have always been Mowafa. And now I was that to the rest of the world, too. I am the first son and first child of Said Househ and Hanan Ghnaim, and I was named Said for my father. This is the custom in our culture: a father's first name becomes the middle name of his children, be they sons or daughters. The practice serves to identify one's paternal lineage, and it goes back to the earliest times, when Arabs were primarily nomads, at home in the desert. Following this tradition, I named my first son Said, after my father. I had wanted to name one of my daughters Hanan, after my mother, but she objected. She thinks that you only name your child after your parent or brother once they pass away (God forbid).

Like many Arab Muslims, my mother kept her own surname after her marriage. When she became pregnant, her sister-in-law—Khadija, who was married to my Uncle Faisal—made sure that she received the traditional pregnancy rituals: herbal tea, chicken soup, and warm molasses, all served by Aunt Khadija to celebrate the start of their new family in northern Alberta.

I was born on 7 December 1977, at Edmonton's Royal Alexandra Hospital. It was the same day that Gordie Howe scored his one-thousandth goal, against the Birmingham Bulls. My father, then working as a travelling giftware salesman, was in High Level, about 750 kilometres north of Edmonton. He found out about my birth the following day. When he arrived back home, the first thing my father did was recite the *athan* in my ear: "There is no god but God, and Muḥammad is the messenger of God."

This profession of faith holds a powerful sense of belonging—to God and to a community of close to two a billion people that transcends national and ethnic boundaries yet shares a spiritual sense of place. The *shahada* ("I bear witness that there is no deity [none truly to be worshipped] but, Allah, and I bear witness that Muḥammad is the messenger of Allah") is the fundamental tenet of the Islamic faith. It forms part of the call to prayer, the *adhan*, which draws Muslims to a place of worship five times each day: *fajr* (dawn), *dhuhr* (midday), *asr* (late afternoon), *maghrib* (shortly after sunset), and *isha* (when total darkness falls). Broadcast from loudspeakers high atop mosques, these calls reach out to the community, bringing everyone together, all turning to face the Kaaba, the holiest of places in Islam that is located near the centre of the Masjid al-Haram, the Great Mosque in the Holy City of Mecca. In some places, like deserts or Prairies, the call to prayer can be heard from far, far away. It is a cinematic cliché—a minaret silhouetted against the early dawn sky, the lonely voice of the muezzin echoing across the soundtrack, an evocation of the exotic, the unknown. But, in the opening credits of my own life, my father spoke the *shahada* to me to wish peace upon my life, to honour my potential and our growth as a

Muslim family—a Palestinian family—trying to stay warm in an Edmonton December.

When my father held me for the first time in Edmonton, I was an anonymous Palestinian Canadian baby waiting for the honour of being named. Like many fathers, he thought hard about naming me Muhammad. Instead, he chose Mowafaq, the name of my mother's brother who had passed away a few months earlier. I've never learned the full story, but Uncle Mowafaq had been involved with a paramilitary group rumoured to be affiliated with Yasser Arafat's Fatah, the dominant faction within the Palestine Liberation Organization and had ended up in exile in Sweden. Uncle Mowafaq died in nebulous circumstances in a car accident in Sweden. The official version of his death is that the brakes on his car accidentally failed, but my family remain convinced that Uncle Mowafaq was killed under mysterious circumstances. My grandmother always claimed his death was linked to Israeli intelligence services operations, but this has never been confirmed.

As individuals, Palestinians may be treated politely, but collectively we are regarded as terrorists, the "unwanted" or the "undesirables." We belong to an invented race, a people defined not by bloodlines but by faith, our piety routinely mistaken for militancy. Rarely are we recognized as displaced persons, as uprooted families searching for an escape, people trying to cope with the pain of survival in an ongoing genocide. As Palestinians, we must defend our right to a future. We come from a nation now deemed to be imaginary, a nation blamed for its stubborn refusal to acquiesce in the face of its own destruction.

In 1993, when I went to apply for my birth certificate at an Alberta registry office in Edmonton, I was told that I could not list "Palestine" as my parents' place of birth. This was not an option. So what was I was supposed to say—that my parents were born in Israel? That would not be true. I realized then that I was up against more than just the anti-Muslim racism of particular individuals. This was a legal form of persecution, with institutions conspiring to erase us from the map.

My name, Mowafa Said Househ, ties me to my family and to Palestine. That is something no one can take from me.

My father became a refugee before he could walk. It was sometime in the summer of 1948, but family memory is vague on the exact dates. Without radio, news came on the night wind of a brutal massacre in the village of Deir Yassin, on the outskirts of Jerusalem. Families attacked in their homes. Bodies everywhere, some mutilated. Women and children killed. In Lydda, where my family is from, people tried to calm each other. "Maybe the stories are wrong. Maybe it was just a few bad soldiers who did things they're not supposed to do. Maybe it's all been exaggerated." But others were whispering, "No, it was a massacre. There is no hope. We could be next."

Rumour was that the attack had been carried out by two Zionist paramilitary organizations, Irgun and Lehi. Not long afterward, fighting broke out in Jaffa, on the coast just south of Tel Aviv and barely twenty kilometres from Lydda. By mid-May, the city was under the control of Israeli forces, and some forty thousand Palestinians had fled, some by land and some by sea. Lydda and the neighbouring town of Ramle, both strategically important towns in the war, lay just off the main road connecting Tel Aviv and Jaffa to Jerusalem and were clearly in Israel's sights.

Fearing another slaughter like the one in Deir Yassin, my grandparents gathered their nine children together and fled their home on foot. Along with many of their neighbours, they trudged east down the dusty road towards the front lines of Jordan's

Arab Legion. "It's just for now, it's just for now," people told each other. "We will go back when it's all been sorted out." Yet, under the unforgiving sun, and in the occasional shade of an olive grove, they could feel the despair. Later, they learned that some Palestinians who had remained in Lydda, including my fourteen-year-old uncle, Darwish, had fought back. Darwish had survived, but other members of their family had died fighting occupation. My great-grandfather, Abdulrahman, had been killed while he was transporting weapons from Turkey to fight against the British. Someone from Lydda communicated his whereabouts to the British, and he was killed. My family's blood has been spilled for Palestine from the earliest days of occupation.

The Israeli occupation of Lydda and Ramle was followed by expulsion orders that were signed on 12 July 1948 and given to the Israel Defense Forces by Lieutenant Colonel Yitzhak Rabin. The orders stated that the inhabitants had to be expelled immediately, no matter how old or young. In the end, perhaps as many as seventy thousand Palestinians were forced to leave the area, joining roughly three-quarters of a million other Palestinian refugees who had fled or been driven out of their towns during the war, and before. Some died from dehydration or from sheer exhaustion during the exodus. Others never even made it that far. They were shot point-blank by Israeli forces for refusing to hand over money and valuables. This massive displacement of Palestinians came to be known as Al-Nakba, the Catastrophe.

The Nakba is soaked into my father's being. His first real home was a leaky tent in a refugee camp in Amman, which lay at the end of the road after the flight from Lydda. My grandfather's brother, Uncle Issa, took refuge in the Gaza Strip, a decision he would come to regret as the violence there escalated. My grandfather and his family initially joined Uncle Issa in Gaza, but then my grandfather decided it would be safer to move to Jordan.

My grandparents had heard that it was safe in Amman, and that Jordan was temporarily welcoming Palestinian refugees until the Arab forces liberated Palestine from Israeli hands—which, of course, never happened.

My grandfather's name was Mahmoud. His name, Mahmoud, means "the praised one" or "worthy of reverence," but everyone called him Tuma. Tuma had been a farmer in Lydda. He had also worked as a farmer and nighttime security guard during the British occupation of Palestine. He owned a home—his own land. When I close my eyes, I can imagine him, tall and proud, and hear his voice. He was in his early thirties in 1948 when he was forced to abandon his land, and his independence abruptly gave way to vulnerability.

As a refugee in Jordan, Tuma found work as a gardener, turning the earth with his hands to feed his family. Whenever he could, he shared generously with his neighbours, giving them the choice of the produce he was able to procure. A humble and pious man, my grandfather looked only to plant new roots in this foreign land and to raise his family with love and give them a secure future.

The call to prayer was deep within my grandfather. Every morning, he would pull himself away from the rest of the family and from the warmth of everyone cuddling together in the tent. At times, it was so cold outside that he had to break the surface ice on the water for *wudu*—ablutions before prayer. As the *fajr* prayer left his lips, his breath would float out on the winter dawn, rooting him in his faith amid loss and upheaval.

I recall my father telling me that story during our family reunion in Calgary in 2013. He agreed that evening before dinner to let me record some of his stories, so I can still hear his scratchy voice share the experiences of his parents, and how his voice aches when he relates the death of one of his brothers in 1960.

When Uncle Faisal, who was working in Germany at the time, heard that Uncle Assad had been diagnosed with leukemia, he arranged for him to come to Germany and stay with him so that he could care for him and take care of any expenses. My dad remembered watching as Tuma hugged Assad and said, "Son, take care of yourself. I fear I will never see you again." Assad died a few weeks later in a German hospital.

My grandparents wept together but accepted that Uncle Assad's death was God's will. They refused to bury their son in Germany. It had to be Palestine. If it couldn't be Lydda, then at least it could be somewhere in the West Bank, an area then under Jordanian control. They chose Nabi Musa, in the desert wilderness south of Jericho—the site of the tomb of the prophet Moses. It was, they said, "a good place for Assad to rest." Just seven years later, his grave would lie in Israeli-occupied territory.

After burying his son, Tuma returned to Jordan. He thought often of Palestine, the only real home he had known—the place where his father, Darwish, his grandfather, Abdulrahman, and his great-grandfather, Khalil, were born. The land of abundance had been ripped apart by the war, and Tuma dreamt how he and his neighbours lived once again like nomads, in tents. He hoped there would be better days ahead for families like theirs.

3

A Circle of Tears

When I was in my early twenties, I travelled to Palestine to seek my own roots under the Nakba tree. As I sought to understand the trail of sorrow my grandparents walked, I found my journal filling up with stories about family ties. Together, the Palestinian territories cover an area only slightly larger than Prince Edward Island. Wherever you go, if you ask about a name, you're likely to find someone who will lead you to the person or family you are looking for. In this way, I met many people who were related to either my father or my mother. I felt a sense of belonging that had always eluded me in Canada, a home in which I often felt like an unwelcome guest.

My time in Palestine coincided with the start of the Second Intifada in September 2000. I spent a week in Hebron, visiting my cousin Reham and her husband, Youssef. Situated about thirty kilometres south of Jerusalem, Hebron lies in the occupied West Bank and has long been a flashpoint in the Israeli-Palestinian conflict. Several years before I arrived, the city had been divided into two zones, with the Israeli Army in control of about a fifth of the territory and the rest administered by the Palestinian Authority (PA). Virtually the entire population is Palestinian—more than

200,000 people, roughly 30,000 of whom live in the Israeli zone. The Jewish settlers, who number well under a thousand, live under military guard, surrounded by Palestinians.

While I was in Hebron, I ended up serving as a translator for a Canadian photographer and an Irish journalist. In the old quarter of the city, with its crumbling city walls, we talked to one of the many families who had been living under Israeli curfew since Ariel Sharon's visit to the Haram esh-Sharif, or Temple Mount as it is known in English. They face food shortages, inadequate access to health services, and no garbage removal. Schools were closed, and some had been taken over by the Israeli Defense Forces for use as military bases. We asked a young man named Ashraf how he was coping under these conditions.

"I'm married and I have a little boy," he said. "I can't work, and I can't buy medicine for my child. I feel helpless because I must support two families. But we are getting used to these conditions; this is not the first time that this has happened. It happened during the First Intifada, too, but this time the rules are much stricter—the soldiers and the settlers are even more violent."

Ashraf was my age, twenty-two. "A year and a half ago," he told us, "I was imprisoned for three months, and no one knew where I was. My family found out where I was when they were contacted to come and fetch me after my release. The soldiers and settlers beat, tortured, and humiliated me. Before they took me to prison, they blindfolded me, tied me up, and placed me in the middle of a crowd of Israeli settlers. I was tied down, and people who walked by me would curse at me and call me a 'Dirty Arab,' then either kick me, slap me, or spit at me. They would feed me food that was repulsive. Sometimes I would watch the settlers as they fed their dogs in pretty glass plates with good food. They played with the dog and nurtured it as I sat there watching. I would at times wish I were that dog. But what can we do? We have adapted to this way of life."

Ashraf's mother was less reconciled to their situation. "He is my only son," she said. "In any other country, the only son is treated well because he is the sole provider for the family. But not here. Not here. We have no money; our food supplies are dwindling. There are some good people who sometimes put meat and vegetables in front of the house. But we can't live like this forever!"

She and her extended family—fifteen people in all—were huddled together in a cramped living space. They lived in a neighbourhood that was often by Israeli forces, and curfews were frequently at all hours of the day. Anyone found on the street after one o'clock in the afternoon, she said, would be beaten or arrested, but she and other family members sometimes took the risk to get medicine or milk for the children.

"I never send my son out for errands," Ashraf's mother told us. "I go instead because I know that if the soldiers catch my son, they will do horrible things to him. My son, my only son, Ashraf, has been arrested many times, and he has been beaten, imprisoned, and humiliated by both the settlers and the soldiers. I am a widow; he's my only son. If anything happens to him, the family will have no other means to survive."

Her voice rose and cracked before she burst into tears. I understood the words, but I groped for some way to translate what she was saying. *This could have been my family,* I kept thinking. *This woman could have been my mother, and I the son who has been abused and thrown into prison. Or she could be Grandma Nima, and the young man my father.* Everyone was a captive here. Unable to speak evenly, I caught my breath and glanced at the journalist and photographer. "I have asthma," I explained. I do have asthma, but that wasn't the problem in this moment.

The stifling atmosphere broke slightly when Ashraf took us for a tour on the roof. "You see how we place cement brick barriers around the water tanks to protect them from bullets,"

Ashraf pointed out. "Improvising, even with the basics." I could see the bullet holes in the cement blocks. My mind flashed to my father's childhood, when his family needed water, and I thought of him later in life, when he worked in a cement factory and then in sales. Standing there on that rooftop listening to Ashraf and his mother speak, the past, the present, and imagined futures all blurred together.

Only weeks before I visited Hebron in October 2000, Muhammad al-Durrah died in the Gaza Strip. He was twelve years old. Caught in the middle of heavy crossfire, he and his father, Jamal, were filmed by a Palestinian cameraman as they crouched behind a concrete barrel set against a concrete wall, both of them clad in jeans and scuffed-up sneakers. In the clip, Jamal reaches out an arm, trying to shield his son, who is sobbing, terror-stricken. Jamal waves frantically. There is a swirl of dust, and Muhammad lies dead across his father's legs.

This brief clip became highly controversial. Was Muhammad really dead? skeptics asked. And, if he was, then how do we know it was Israeli soldiers who shot him? Was the entire sequence staged? Detailed investigations and ballistics reports followed, with Israelis claiming that it was all a plot to defame the country, and Palestinians reacting with outrage to such allegations. In an atmosphere of bitter polarization, finding the "truth" acquires an exaggerated meaning. It was as if the legitimacy of the entire Palestinian struggle depended on the authenticity of this one image.

There are countless other images, two-dimensional snaps of this reality that is three generations deep. Fathers and mothers cradling their children, victims of rocket attacks on Gaza, whether in 2000, or 2006, 2014, or 2021. Kids pierced and burned by shrapnel, rushed into overburdened hospitals. Family portraits of smiling faces covered in concrete dust in the rubble of living rooms. While I was in Palestine, I would often—too often—hear parents cry on the news, "What did my child do to die like this? What was his mistake? She was eleven months old . . . He was five years old . . . She was twelve years old . . . What did they do?"

Those voices have echoed in my head from the day I first heard them. In December 2013, when my family gathered in Calgary, I was about to become the father to my third child. After our dinner table conversation, my father had agreed to let me record his stories—for me, and for his children's children. I held my mobile phone recording device close to preserve my father's voice, hoping somehow to liberate him from the exhaustion weighing on his spirit. I did not know then that, only eight months later—right in the middle of the International Year of Solidarity with the Palestinian People—Gaza would experience a summer of almost inconceivable destruction that would kill more than 2,250 members of my extended family, including 550 children. According to the United Nations Human Rights Council's *Report of the Independent Commission of Inquiry on the 2014 Gaza Conflict*, some 11,230 people were wounded, 30 percent of them children; eighteen thousand homes were obliterated. Blood would be shed at checkpoints, and our people would die beneath concrete chunks of their broken homes. The violence would split our hearts across hemispheres.

Living in exile, we try to find some way to heal from the sorrows of displacement. We do our best to come to come to terms with our situation, to cross beyond the physical and mental checkpoints that prevent us from accessing our new home and a new identity fully, or from returning to our ancestral homes. But it is not easy to heal when the wounds are constantly reopened.

EAST

الشرق

4

The Price of Slippers

"Yama, I feel sick."

"What's wrong, Said? What would make you feel better?"

"If I have some meat, then I'll feel a lot better."

My father tells the story in the present tense, as if no time has elapsed between his childhood and this moment in Calgary. Time is fluid when you live in the intermediate state of exile and memory.

When her son said things like that, my grandmother would go out to the local store and buy some canned luncheon meat on credit. Young Said would wolf it down straight out of the can, closing his eyes in ecstasy. Sometimes he'd eat it so fast that he actually *would* feel sick. When he was a little older, he would occasionally get a treat so special that it came as a shock. The creamy sweetness of a ripe banana, or the rich, melting flavour of chocolate that lingers on your tongue. But that came even later.

When I was ten, I won a reading competition at school and was rewarded with a voucher for a three-pound bar of chocolate from World's Finest. Eager and anxious, I looked for my prize in the mail every day, but it never arrived. I complained about the unfairness of it all, and that was when my father told me that he was about fifteen before he ever tasted chocolate. I still felt cheated, but not in the same way that he was.

When my father's family arrived in Jordan, they were given tents and shown to land that had been set aside for refugees. In 1952, that informal settlement became known officially as Jabal el-Hussein. It was one of several refugee camps set up in Jordan in the wake of Al-Nakba by UNRWA—the United Nations Relief and Works Agency for Palestine Refugees in the Near East. Until he was six, my father's home was a tent, where the family slept like tinned fish, huddled together for warmth, some kicking in their sleep, or crying out, or whimpering, "Still hungry, Yaba . . . Yama." Whenever water leaked into the tent, someone would get up and try to find a sheet of plastic to pull over them. Or else everyone would move, grumbling, to another part of the tent that seemed a little drier.

As a young child, Said was carried around on his older brothers' shoulders, and tossed from one to the other like a football. There were disagreements and fights, as in any family, but they were together—especially at night. They spent five years in that tent before they were able to get a house. Finally, they had four walls and some protection from the elements. But not from hunger. This was a time when the family had meat only once a week, a small piece for each of them. Dinner was more likely to be some combination of cooked vegetables, rice, bread, olive oil with cheese, all sprinkled with za'atar, a mixture of oregano and other herbs and roasted sesame seeds. Often, there wasn't enough, and many nights Said and his family went to sleep with empty stomachs. "But we loved each other," my father told me. "We all ate at the same time, when we had food, and we never fought over it."

As he grew older, Said began to assert himself. He was the only one of the children who was constantly getting into trouble, sparking the stories of how his brothers brought back the wrong baby—a bad, naughty baby—from under the Nakba tree.

By the time my father was a teenager, the tents supplied by UNRWA when the first refugees arrived after the Nakba had given way to more permanent structures, mostly constructed by the refugees themselves, and with UNRWA contributing materials for roofing. Yet Jabal el-Hussein was still known as a refugee camp, and my father was deeply embarrassed when his better-off acquaintances found out where he lived. *I have to cover up*, he thought. *I have to be someone I'm not, something better.*

Throughout my father's childhood, war was never far away. Said was aware of the activities of Palestinian resistance fighters, including the founding of Fatah and then of the Palestine Liberation Organization, but he had other things to think about. Often, he was more worried about his reputation than about the war zone in which he lived, so he would make sure that his friends picked him up somewhere else—away from the camp. He would make his way to a better neighbourhood on foot and stand casually in front of some nice-looking building, waiting for them to show up—trying to protect an identity fabricated by shame.

As he could seldom afford a taxi for the return trip home, my father would walk back to the refugee camp along the dirt roads, often in the rain. Along the way, he would be splashed by passing vehicles as they tried to take shortcuts. Seeing his muddy clothes and shoes, Grandma Nima would yell, "Not again! We just did the washing!" He always had the same excuse: He'd been play-fighting with his friends. She would click her tongue with frustration as he tracked mud across the floor. She tried hard to keep their simple home tidy, especially in case neighbours visited.

One day, he slipped and tore his only pair of pants. They could not be repaired, and his family had no money. He was forced to wear a pair of red pantaloons that belonged to one of his sisters for a week, until my grandfather was able to find a little extra cash to buy him a used pair of men's trousers.

Although he was a bit of a rebel, my dad was intelligent and determined. Education was the only hope for any kind of future. There was something pushing him not to be left behind. At fourteen, he was working at Al-Shaksheer Pharmacy in downtown Amman, cleaning and helping the pharmacist. The owner noticed him and said, "You're smart—why don't you study to become a pharmacy assistant?"

My father enrolled at a local college in Amman and studied hard, earning his diploma in pharmacy at the age of nineteen. At the time in Amman, according to my father, there was no official college of pharmacy. His licence to practice pharmacy hangs in my office till this day. He walked about seven kilometres a day between school, work, and home. It was enough to put holes in shoes that were not durable to begin with, but he and his family learned to make sandals out of pieces of rubber cut from tires, bound together with string. His training at the college was intensive and demanding, but eventually Said became so skilled that he could manage the pharmacy himself, without the supervision of the pharmacist. Grandma Nima would say things like, "I never knew that the youngest one, the troublemaker, would do so well. I guess we got the right baby after all."

Said's achievements gave him a privileged position in his world. Although many of the people in the camp were accustomed to relying on folk remedies, such as *maramia* tea or coffee infused with roasted cumin, or bloodletting—still quite common tradition in Islamic culture—they started coming to him for help when they were sick or in need of medication. Many could not afford prescriptions or a consultation with a physician but Said could get medicines for free or at a cheaper rates through his work. My father never turned anyone away, and my grandfather Tuma was proud of him for that. "Here he is!" people in the camp would say when they saw him. "Come in, come in … drink some coffee."

One day, a perfume company gave Said hundreds of samples to distribute to pharmacy customers. Instead, he took the samples to the refugee camp and handed them out to neighbours, friends, and family. He kept some of the samples for himself and poured them into a bucket so he could wash his feet in perfumed water. "I did this so I could feel, for a short time, that I was doing something I thought rich people would do," he told me. For weeks, the fragrance of perfume mingled with the heavy odours of the camp.

My father remembered an earlier time, too, when another luxury arrived in the camp, "What is this sound? Where is it from?" People would gather, eager and curious. My dad and his brother Faisal had saved up to buy a radio, paying for it in instalments. "At night we listened to the Cairo radio station, knowing that we could go to jail if we were found out." Egypt's socialist president, Gamal Abdel Nasser, was no friend of monarchies, or of religious people, for that matter, and his growing popularity in the Arab world posed a threat to Jordan's King Hussein, who was frequently criticized on Voice of the Arabs. The Cairo-based station broadcast throughout much of the Arab world, spreading Nasser's calls for Arabic unity in the face of imperialism and messages of support for the liberation of Palestine. "We took a few risks," Dad said in his understated manner, "and it helped the boredom to hear those distant voices." A few risks—their curiosity could easily have landed them in prison.

Jabal el-Hussein was one of four refugee camps in Jordan. All of them were densely populated seas of makeshift tents filled with families fighting for some sort of life. The Jordanian government was working to bring sanitation, water, and electricity into these impoverished areas, which gradually evolved into urban villages. "There were always people like your grandfather and father," Uncle Faisal told me, "trying to provide some extra food or money for those worse off. But there were also local drunkards, as well as thieves, cheats, and other criminals. It made it hard to raise a family in any normal way."

Most of the stories about my family's years in the El-Hussein camp came from Uncle Faisal. Until he passed away in 2006, he was like a second father to me, someone who could help me understand my father's silences. He had an almost photographic memory and was near the top of his class in secondary school in Jordan. When he was young, he also wrote poems and stories, including one called *Al-Fata* Al Muazab (The Tormented Child), about a child living n a refugee camp. One of his poems, in which he praised King Hussein, was made into a song and played at a local radio station. "I had to write that poem," he said. "After all, we could have been in trouble, your dad and me, listening to Cairo radio and insulting the king who had offered us safety."

In another time and place, Uncle Faisal could have been a physician or scholar. But my grandfather sat him down one day and said, "Faisal, you are one of my most reliable sons. I need you to quit school to work and help the family."

"Yes, Yaba. I understand."

The school principal was terribly upset and came to the house to plead with Tuma to let Uncle Faisal continue his studies. But the family was growing and there were nine children to feed now. So my uncle began to apprentice as a carpenter. In 1960, when he was seventeen, Uncle Faisal went to Germany with his brother, my uncle Saleh, to work in a mine—contract jobs that paid well. This was a turning point in our family's life. The money they sent home from Germany meant that my grandfather didn't have to work as hard himself and could focus instead on building a new home. There were jokes about "Faisal the carpenter, helping build the house from a distance." But, for my grandfather, it was another step away from memories of that leaky UNRWA tent.

≪ · ≫

When I travelled to Palestine in 2000, I made a trip to Amman to visit my relatives and to recover some of the memories I had of living there with my parents between 1985 and 1988, when I was still young. Originally built on seven hills, Amman had expanded rapidly during the second half of the twentieth century, opening its arms to waves of refugees from Palestine, Kuwait, and Iraq. More recently, they had come from Syria. A lot had happened since I had lived there, and my perspective was different.

I wandered through the souks and masjids of Al-Balad, the old downtown area that sits in a valley next to a hill called Jabal Amman. There on the hill, not far from the fancy shops, the cafés, clubs, and restaurants, and the elegant hotels that cluster around the main traffic circle, is the old refugee camp where thousands of Palestinians still live, many in conditions not much better than those in which my father's family lived. One often finds these stark contrasts between rich and poor, and not only in the Middle East.

The El-Hussein camp is a congested ghetto filled with run-down, ramshackle houses jammed together in narrow, dirty lanes. The houses overflow with families, the roads are crowded, traffic gets snarled, and sometimes sewage runs down open ditches. Approaching Amman by air, you can spot the camp with ease by looking for the countless piles of bricks placed on top of flimsy roofs to prevent them from flying away in a strong wind. In the local markets, tiny neon-lit shops do their business beneath a naked forest of power poles and lines, many of which carry no electricity. Your senses can be overwhelmed by the noise and stench that is occasionally punctuated by the aroma of strong Arabic coffee, honey-laden sweets, and freshly baked flatbread.

In 2000, I was about the same age my father was when he was embarking on life as a pharmacy assistant. I'd visited El-Hussein several times already, but I had a special errand for which

I needed my cousin Muhammad as a guide. Making our way through a maze of lanes, we found the house I was looking for. Muhammad and I knocked on the door and a young girl, about eight years old, opened it just a little and peered at us through the crack. She asked us who we were and what it was we wanted.

"My name is Mowafa Said Househ," I said, "and I would like to see the place where my grandparents, uncles, and father once lived." I had brought some groceries with me, which I handed to her.

Hesitantly, she accepted the gift. "Please can you wait?" She called her mother, who came to the door and asked the same questions her daughter had asked. I answered them again.

"Ahlan wa sahlan!" she said, smiling. "Welcome!"

I stepped inside at the invitation, but my cousin Muhammad hung back. It was obvious that he didn't want to go in. The cramped single storey rowhouse house was built out of cement blocks around a small shared open courtyard where my father and his brothers had once played, just like I did growing up in Edmonton. But that was the end of the resemblance: it seemed impossible to bridge the gap between their reality and my own.

I looked around the tiny house and imagined Grandma Nima calling her husband and children to get ready for supper. My father had told me that they all ate from the same plate and often did not have enough—but that they shared what they had. My eyes burned as I thought of their life here. After ten minutes or so, I thanked the kind woman with more smiles and left. She would never know how much that visit meant to me or how strongly I felt a connection to my grandparents during that brief glimpse into their lives.

Muhammad and I continued to walk through the neighbour-hood shops and markets, but I noticed that he was unusually quiet. At a shoe store, I looked at some slippers priced at two Jordanian dinars—about $3.50 at the time. Afterwards, we stopped for lunch at one of my favourite places, a kebab house called Inta Umri, where I already knew I could get the best kebabs and *arayes* in Mukhayyam el-Hussein. It was run by a family friend, Muhammad al-Dabash, who'd owned it for more than forty years. He had known my grandparents and my father. As hard as I tried over the days I was there, I could not get information from him. Today was no different. He kept deflecting my questions.

"I have come thousands of miles," I persisted.

He waved me away. "Enjoy it! Enjoy it!" he urged, as he pushed the kebabs, *arayes*, and grilled vegetables over to me.

After Muhammad and I finished our lunch, we took a taxi to an upscale mall in downtown Amman. I could tell he was glad to be out of the refugee camp. Inside the mall, all shining and noisy and new, I wandered into one of the shoe stores. There were Nikes and Adidas, and, to my surprise, the same slippers I'd seen earlier. I asked the salesman the price.

"Ten dinars."

"Why are they so expensive?"

My cousin looked agitated. The salesman launched into an explanation of why the slippers deserved such a price. But I wanted to say my piece. "Just so you know, I found these same slippers in the El-Hussein refugee camp for two dinars."

Muhammad abruptly walked away.

I followed Muhammad outside the mall and into a taxi. He refused to look at me and wanted me to sit in the front of the cab. Although I could guess the answer, I asked him, "What's the matter with you? Why are you so angry?"

"How could you embarrass us like that—telling him we were at the refugee camp, shopping? They might think we lived there! They'll talk!" He glared at me.

"I don't care what they think or what you think. It is where my father grew up."

33

He kept quiet, still fuming as the taxi took us through the narrow, congested streets, all the way to his home in a nicer middleclass neighbourhood of the city.

When we arrived home, Muhammad stormed inside. His mother asked me what had happened. I told her the story, and she laughed at his reaction. But Muhammad's sister and brother quickly stepped in to defend him, trying to explain how important status is in their culture and how people are judged by where they shop and who they know.

"Here, people care a lot about our historical roots, you know!" they said. And it is true. Everyone we met always asked about our lineage, right up to my great-great grandparents. Such knowledge doesn't define how people see you, but it does give them a context within which to place you and your family. In other words, if my lineage revealed that my grandparents were collaborating with the Israelis or the English, that label would haunt me for generations. Since almost all Palestinians in Jordan started off living in the refugee camps, and those who made it out of the camps are regarded as successful and affluent. Only the poor and miserable remain in the camps. I did not fully appreciate at the time how my actions could affect my family who lived in Amman.

"The issue isn't Jordanian culture," I retorted. "It's your own shame at being associated with the refugee camp. But your father and mother lived there, and some of you were actually born and grew up there."

They were furious.

As I thought about my response to Muhammad's behaviour, I realized that I had been arrogant and insensitive. I had forgotten what I knew about life in a refugee camp, about the way it stains your life. "Nothing could be more precarious than that—maybe one day you will understand it, the kind of place I grew up in," Uncle Faisal once told me, and my father had said similar things over the years. Had Uncle Faisal not helped my family move to Canada, I would have been just like my cousins, living in shame not far from the ghetto of their past, and struggling to hold their heads high. While I visited my family in Jordan and spent time in Palestine, I gradually came to understand that to be Palestinian is to constantly feel displaced, yearning for a place to call home. It is to admit to an identity compromised by loss.

5

Planting Saplings

When I was an undergraduate at the University of Alberta, I met a guy named Mustafa. He spoke with a Lebanese accent, and I asked where he was from. "I am one hundred percent Lebanese," he replied. He asked me the same question, and I told him I was Palestinian. He looked at me. "I don't like Palestinians," he said. "It was because of them that Lebanon was destroyed."

I had heard this before, from Wesam, Aunt Khadija's nephew on her side of the family. Their family had moved to Canada from Lebanon in 1993, when I was still in high school. "You're Palestinian," he said when we first met. "I hate Palestinians." *His aunt is Uncle Faisal's wife,* I thought. *We are basically relatives!* Years later, I asked his father, who was from the Beqaa Valley in Lebanon, why his son would say that. "This is ignorance," he replied. "The Lebanese people blame the Palestinians for their civil war."

Mustafa was not what one would call a model Muslim: he liked to drink beer and flirt. He would tell me stories about late-night parties in Beirut, about his military service, and about his summer job as a tour guide in Lebanon. One day, I ran into him while I was walking to class. He looked at me critically and said, "Mowafa, you're a little *mlazliz*." I was taken aback, but not because he had accused me of being overweight, which is what *mlazliz* means. I was surprised that he knew the word at all.

I told him that I'd never heard anyone use that word except for a couple of my old-fashioned elderly aunts. "Are you sure you don't have any Palestinian blood in you?" I joked.

He was not amused. "Don't be ridiculous," he said. Then he spun around and walked away.

A few months later, I found out from Uncle Yazan Haymour that Mustafa's father was Palestinian. His mother was Lebanese, but he had grown up in Jordan—in Amman, in fact. During the summers, he visited his grandparents in Lebanon, where he faced hostility because his father was Palestinian, and that was probably when he had learned to mask his Palestinian roots by adopting a Lebanese accent.

It seemed sad that even in Canada he felt compelled to deny his own heritage. Again, the shame, the stigma attached to being Palestinian, coupled with the fear of backlash.

In Muslim culture, we are taught that even though another life awaits us after we die, we must never stop doing what is right in this one. In Hadith No. 12491, The Prophet Muḥammad, peace and blessings be upon him, said, "If the Resurrection were established upon one of you while he has in his hand a sapling, then let him plant it." We plant one sapling, and then another, and another, regardless of where we are.

Uncle Faisal was the first of our family to leave the Middle East. He ended up in Edmonton in 1964—one of few Palestinians in the city at the time. He was lucky enough to find lodging with a pious Muslim from Lebanon, Mr. Tarrabain, and his family, who provided him with a home away from home. All the same,

Uncle Faisal would get very emotional every time he spoke with his family over the crackling telephone wires. Back in Jordan, Grandma Nima would burst into tears whenever she heard "Ba'eed Anak" ("Far from You") sung so powerfully by the famed Egyptian contralto, Umm Kulthum.

It was not long before Faisal began to wish for a family of his own, and one day he asked Mrs. Tarrabain if she knew of a good Muslim woman who might be interested in marrying him. Indeed she did. She had a cousin, Khadija, who lived in Saadnayel, a town in the fertile Beqaa Valley in eastern Lebanon. Mrs. Tarrabain showed Uncle Faisal a picture of her cousin, and my uncle agreed to marry her. Introductions ensued by mail, and soon marriage followed. As Uncle Faisal was unable to leave Canada at that time, he sent a family member over to ask for her hand formally and to participate in the required rituals on his behalf. While the ceremonies unfolded in Lebanon, back in Edmonton, my now newly married Uncle Faisal continued working as a night janitor at the Royal Alexandra Hospital.

In 1967, the first Canadian-born Househ child came into the world—my oldest cousin, Hala. The year also saw the birth of the Canadian Arab Federation, formed to represent the interests of the country's growing Arab Canadian communities. And, of course, this was the year of Canada's centennial celebration, complete with Expo '67, a world fair with pavilions for many countries and lands, including Kuwait and the United Arab Republic, as Egypt was known at the time. At the end of May, however, Kuwait closed its pavilion. The mood in the Middle East was not festive.

Palestinians also remember 1967, but not as a year of celebration. It is impossible to explain succinctly what transpired in 1967, but the end result was disastrous for Palestine. In 1950, Jordan had taken control of the area known as Transjordán, or the West Bank—land that the UN General Assembly had earmarked for an independent Arab State in Resolution 181 on 22 November 1947. Tension had been growing since the November 1966, when Israeli troops had marched into the West Bank and attacked the Palestinian village of As Samu' in retaliation for the death of three Israeli police who had been killed when a border patrol vehicle drove over a land mine reportedly planted by Fatah. More than a hundred homes in the village were destroyed, along with a school and a medical clinic. Nearly twenty people died in the attack, including three civilians.

Historically, the Sinai Peninsula had been part of Egyptian territory since antiquity; Gaza requires a history of its own. Originally built as an Egyptian fortress in Canaanite territory during the time of the pharaohs, it had a history of being occupied by invading forces. After the First World War, the Gaza Strip—Gaza City and the surrounding land—became part of the British Mandated Territory. In 1948, Egypt took over de facto governance of the Gaza Strip until 1967. In May 1967, Egypt— reacting to what it believed was Israeli mobilization along the Syrian border, across from the Golan Heights—closed the Straits of Tiran to Israeli shipping, thereby barring Israeli access to the Red Sea via the Gulf of Aqaba. Israel was swift to respond to Nasser's action. On 5 June, Israeli planes bombed Egyptian airfields, essentially wiping out the Egyptian air force, while ground forces simultaneously launched attacks in the Sinai and the Gaza Strip. After Syria and Jordan entered the fray in support of Egypt, Israel invaded Syria's Golan Heights, and seized East Jerusalem and the West Bank.

The consequences for Palestine were devastating. When the war ended on 10 June 1967, the Sinai Peninsula, the Gaza Strip, and large swathes of the West Bank were under Israeli control, and roughly a million Palestinians now lived in Occupied Territory.

In the aftermath of the war, entire Palestinian villages in the West Bank were razed, and two refugee camps in the vicinity of Jericho were "emptied" by forcing the refugees out of their places of refuge. By the end of the year, some three hundred thousand Palestinians had fled the territories taken by Israel—Palestinians were on the move yet again, their worldly possessions wrapped up in bundles and carried on their heads. Throats parched, they stumbled wearily through the desert, taking shelter in caves where they risked being bitten by snakes and scorpions. From there, they watched the night skies light up with falling bombs. Uprooted families—many for the second time—huddled together in tents as they faced an unknown future, their dreams broken by the rumbling of explosions.

The invasion occurred less than twenty years after Al-Nakba, but this new disaster was not a final defeat. This second exodus came to be called Al-Naksa—the Setback. By December 1967, and beyond, hundreds of thousands of Palestinians were fleeing from the West Bank and Gaza to Jordan and Egypt, or from the Golan Heights further into Syria. While Palestinians in the now-occupied territories fled their homes, Uncle Faisal and his wife, Khadija, set up their home in Edmonton, Alberta. A world away, my father and his family continued their struggle to survive in an increasingly crowded refugee camp in Amman. Occasionally, news filtered through about Faisal in Canada, a place many of members of my family, including my father, would try to make their new home. So they learned that after working as a janitor, Uncle Faisal had started his own giftware business, and was working as a travelling salesman selling oil paintings and other gift items. He was in a better position financially, but it meant that he was away from Edmonton and his growing family for weeks at a time.

Uncle Faisal didn't just take care of his family in Canada, but like a good son and observant Muslim, he continued to send money to his family who had been displaced by the Nakba and who needed help. Palestinian exiles, like members of many other diasporic communities, do not forget their relatives living in less fortunate circumstances.

Despite the pressures of his job, Uncle Faisal was active in Edmonton's Muslim community in the 1970s and 1980s, by which time the faith community had grown to about sixteen thousand. Uncle Faisal was also a Muslim who said what he meant, often not troubling to soften his words. It had been rough in the refugee camps. "Nothing could be more precarious than that," he told me. "Maybe one day you will know it, the kind of place I grew up in."

My father had said similar things over the years, referring to the camp as a kind of cancer on the structure of life that had made him what he was. Often, it explained things he saw as flaws or shortcomings in himself.

While my uncle settled into his new life in Canada, my grandfather and his family in Amman watched as history repeated itself, not realizing what history was still to come. They thought about Uncle Faisal, now living far away, married and a father, and how he seemed to be finding some financial stability. The loss of the West Bank had dealt a crippling blow to the Jordanian economy, and the city of Amman was increasingly crowded, not only with yet more refugees, but with Palestinian freedom fighters who had shifted their operations from the West Bank into Jordan. They were soon joined by fedayeen from Syria and Lebanon, and Jordan became the PLO's new home.

Groups within the PLO shared a purpose—the liberation of Palestine from Israeli control and the restoration of Palestinian self-rule. Little unity existed, however, as far as tactics went. While many fedayeen were affiliated with Yasser Arafat's Fatah, many belonged to other more radical groups—the largest and most influential of which was the PFLP, the Popular Front for the Liberation of Palestine, founded in 1967 by George Habash, who came from my grandfather's village of Lydda. During the late 1960s, the fedayeen became an increasingly bold presence in Jordan, weakening King Hussein's control over the country. Violent clashes were occurring between PLO groups and the Jordanian Army, and yet Hussein was reluctant to deal too harshly with the fedayeen, since they enjoyed the support of much of the Arab world.

By the summer of 1970, the PFLP was openly calling for the overthrow of King Hussein, as were several other groups. In June, violence erupted at Zarqa, a town not far northeast of Amman, and shortly after that fedayeen attacked the Jordanian intelligence headquarters in Amman. As King Hussein was on his way to the scene, fedayeen opened fire on his motorcade in an assassination attempt that killed one of his guards. Almost immediately, several Army units responded by shelling both El-Hussein and Al-Wehdat, the other Palestinian refugee camp in Amman.

My father was working in Kuwait at the time, so he did not experience the chaos that engulfed the refugee camp first-hand, as my grandfather and the rest of the family did. The battle went on for three days and left some three hundred people dead. Despite negotiations between Arafat and Hussein, no resolution was in sight. At the start of September, fighting broke out in Amman after another attempt was made on Hussein's life. But it was the PFLP's airplane hijackings about a week later—ironically intended to draw fiery attention to the Palestinian cause—that sealed the fate of the PLO in Jordan. In mid-September, the Jordanian Army began shelling the two refugee camps again, and this time the battle lasted for ten days. Even after a ceasefire agreement was signed, the PFLP and another radical group, the Democratic Front for the Liberation of Palestine, refused to give up the fight, and as a result the fedayeen were driven out of Jordan by the following summer—mostly into Lebanon, which now replaced Jordan as the PLO's new home.

My uncles and aunts fled to Aunt Khadija's hometown of Saadnayel in Lebanon's Beqaa Valley with their families and my grandmother. My father and one of my aunts stayed behind in Jordan to protect the new house he had recently built in Jabal al-Nuzha from possible looters. He and my aunt describe the civil war of 1970 and 1971 as probably the most terrifying period of their lives. Once again, my family was dispersed and had to struggle to make a new home in a foreign land.

After the Al-Naksa, our family dispersed even further than before. Uncle Faisal came to Canada, Uncle Muhammad found work in Iraq, and my father worked in Kuwait. Yet no matter how busy their lives got, or how far they spread across the globe, they kept in touch. As things settled, the family came to a joint decision about their future. For the sake of the whole family, they decided, Said should come to Canada, along with his brother Muhammad, and that Faisal should sponsor them. Having decided on a course of action, Said and Muhammad came to Canada. Once in Canada, my father soon discovered that his credentials as a pharmacy assistant were worthless. Despite his hard-earned diploma and his years of experience, he ended up working in a cement factory. He did not work there for long before he joined Uncle Faisal in his giftware business.

By the time Said was able to return to Jordan for a visit, his father had died. Said had been asked to deliver some gifts to members of his extended family, who lived in Syria. Since there were no flights between Amman and Syria, Said took a taxi to Damascus. When he arrived at their door, Hanan opened it. "It was," he told me, "love at first sight."

Hanan's parents promised Said that they would speak to her about marriage, and he was told to return in a few days for an answer. My father came back bearing many gifts of his own, and he was elated when Hanan's father said, "Ask your family to come and request our daughter's hand." This meant that she had agreed, even though there were more formalities to come.

My eldest uncle, Darwish, and several other members of the family then travelled to Syria to ask for my mother's hand in marriage. As per custom, there was the initial meeting to confirm the agreement by sharing coffee and sweets and making arrangements for the marriage. That was followed a few months later by a small wedding ceremony at his Uncle Issa's home in Jordan, followed by an Egyptian honeymoon. My parents had originally planned to have a big wedding, but shortly after my mother's family arrived in Jordan, they heard that her brother Majid had been killed in an accident in Syria, which meant that her parents had to return home to make arrangements for the funeral. So instead, the close family gathered at Uncle Issa's house to witness the ceremony. There was no music and no food. Afterwards, they took some pictures and went home.

Hanan stayed with her family in Syria while my father returned to Canada to deal with the required paperwork to get my mother to join him. Back in Edmonton, he was so excited and proud that he kept shoving a photograph of his new bride in people's faces, kissing it every few minutes.

After Hanan arrived in Canada in 1975, my parents lived for a year with Uncle Faisal's family. From the beginning, my family members attended Edmonton's Al-Rashid Mosque—the first mosque in Canada, which opened its doors in December

1938. It seems strangely appropriate that these displaced souls would find their spiritual home in a mosque that also has its own history of displacement. The original mosque was built by a Ukrainian Canadian contractor and bore a curious resemblance to an Eastern Orthodox church. It was located right next to Victoria High School, but when the school needed to expand in 1946, the mosque was moved several blocks north to a site near the Royal Alexandra Hospital. By the start of the 1980s, the building had become too small for the city's growing Muslim community, so a new Al-Rashid Mosque was constructed further to the northwest. The old building sat vacant for nearly a decade, until plans for the hospital's expansion threatened it with demolition. Thanks to the efforts of the Canadian Council of Muslim Women, it was saved from destruction, and funds were raised to move the historic building to Fort Edmonton Park.

When I first heard the story of how the mosque was moved, I imagined the mosque being lifted onto a flatbed truck and rolled away by the light of the moon to its new home in the Edmonton river valley. And there the two mosques are today: one in the north end of the city, and one in the river valley beside other historic structures. Displaced and residing in two places at once, much like Palestinians themselves.

6

In the Line of Fire

I was not yet five years old in June 1982 when Israel invaded Lebanon with the intention of putting an end to the PLO's presence in the country. Even at that young age, I could feel the effects of what was happening thousands of miles away. I heard my parents and older family members talking, sometimes anxiously, sometimes angrily. My emotional radar could sense how close this new violence was to my parents' hearts.

Lebanon had been embroiled in a civil war since before I was born, a war that would drag on throughout the 1980s. The political situation in Lebanon had long been unstable—a Maronite Christian elite arrayed against a Muslim majority, some Shi'a, and some Sunni, with the Muslim population then augmented by an influx of Palestinian refugees from the 1948 war. When, at the start of the 1970s, the PLO shifted its base of operations into Lebanon, its presence further destabilized an already precarious balance of power among rival factions, both political and sectarian. In 1975, fighting erupted, with alliances forming and dissolving as the war unfolded.

The Israeli invasion of Lebanon in early June 1982 was accompanied by a new round of heavy bombardment. The attacks lasted for months, provoking international concern that culminated in US intervention. By late August, the PLO had withdrawn to northern Lebanon, and a new president had been installed—Bachir Gemayel, the leader of the Maronite Christian Kataeb Party, commonly called the Phalanges in English. Israel refused to withdraw its troops, however, and, at the start of September, the government of Menachem Begin rejected a peace plan laid out by US president Ronald Reagan. Instead, and in open defiance of the plan, Israel announced its intention to establish seven new settlements in the West Bank and Gaza.

In Edmonton, the rabbi of Beth Sholom synagogue responded to these events by inviting the Arab Muslim community to join him in a discussion of the crisis in Lebanon. The rabbi and his wife were acquainted with Uncle Faisal from multicultural events in the city. As the story is told in our family, Uncle Faisal said little at first, but when the rabbi tried to justify Israel's settlement policy as a form of self-defence, my uncle had had enough of the discussion. As he stood up, the scrape of his chair echoed through the hall. "What you say is wrong! Many innocent civilians are going to die because of Israeli aggression. This war should be stopped immediately, and the Israeli government should be persecuted for this massacre."

Massacre! The rabbi's wife tried to placate my uncle: "Faisal, why are you so angry? You and I share many things. Not eating pork, for instance."

"You may not eat pork," he snapped, "but for years you have eaten the flesh off our children's backs." Then he stormed out to the sound of furious clapping.

Faisal's prediction proved brutally accurate. Lebanon's new president lasted barely three weeks. In mid-September, he and some two dozen others were killed when a bomb exploded at the Kataeb Party headquarters. Although a member of the Syrian

Socialist Nationalist Party was swiftly arrested for planting the bomb, both the Phalangists and the Israelis assumed that Palestinian nationalists were responsible.

Retribution was massive and immediate. The Israeli Defense Forces entered West Beirut and surrounded the Sabra and Shatila refugee camps, providing artillery support while Phalangist militia attacked. The four-hour assault on Sabra and Shatila was more than a massacre. Women were raped and their bodies mutilated; children were butchered and thrown onto garbage piles. It was an atrocity enabled by Israeli troops and committed by right-wing Christians, some of whom carved crosses in the flesh of their victims. The number of victims remains a matter of dispute, but the figure of seven to eight hundred used by Israel's commission of inquiry likely represents about a quarter of the actual total.

About a year after the Israeli invasion of Lebanon, E.T., the extra-terrestrial creature from the Stephen Spielberg film, paid a visit to the Abbottsfield Mall, which was not far from the Beverley neighbourhood where my family lived at the time. I remember going with my mother to the mall and excitedly reaching out to touch E.T.—his wrinkled body, with its skinny neck, huge, piercing blue eyes, and long, thin hand with the glowing fingertip. At the time, I was oblivious to the irony that one of my earliest memories would be of an alien being who struggled to stay alive long enough to return to his homeland.

I also remember a game of tag in our apartment building. I was playing with two brothers, Bashar and Khaldoon, who had come with us to see E.T., and several other children, all of us racing up and down the hallways in the building. Bashar was "it" and he was chasing me and Khaldoon. I was out in front, and at one point I ran through the entrance into another hallway and quickly slammed the door behind me so that Bashar could tag Khaldoon, which he did. I started to laugh, and Khaldoon, who was furious, came after me. He had a plastic straw in his hand, and the last thing I saw was his hand moving towards my face. Suddenly, the world exploded, and I could not see. My eye hurt like nothing had hurt me before. I was screaming and crying, and someone ran into the apartment building to fetch my parents. My father came to see what had happened. It took him only one look at my eye to assess the damage. He grabbed me, threw me in his truck, and headed for the hospital. He was going so fast that he was stopped by the police. My father pointed at me, and the cops then escorted us to the hospital, lights flashing and sirens whooping to clear the way. At any other time, I would have been thrilled.

At the emergency room, the doctor checked my eye, applied some liquid gel, and taped a piece of cotton over it. That night, back home, I snuggled against my mother, terrified that I would lose my eye. "You will be okay, you will be all right," she kept saying, to comfort me. "There's nothing to worry about. We are here. You have too much life ahead of you not to see it!" But as I lay there, I thought about Uncle Faisal, who had lost an eye when someone threw a stone at him in his youth back in the Middle East. He had lost his eye because of that incident and wore a glass eye for the rest of his life. I felt sad that no one had rushed him to a hospital to save his eye. Only when I was older did I realize that Uncle Faisal saw more with his one eye than most people see with both.

Later that year, my father took me to a demonstration against the Israeli bombardment of Lebanon. I sat on my father's shoulders as he marched in downtown Edmonton with hundreds of other community members—there I was, a five-year-old child, happily chanting along with everyone else: "Reagan, Begin, you should know, we support the PLO!"

Although I really had no idea what was going on, I was beginning to understand that I Palestinian as well as Canadian. I had a certain kind of blood, but I spoke English, and not with the heavy accent of my father. When a local political candidate who was in the crowd asked me where I was from, I said the first words that entered my mind: "I'm Palestinian!" He smiled, and so did my father. I felt proud of myself. Apparently, I'd said the right thing.

I was downtown with my father again in the spring of 1984, when the Edmonton Oilers won the Stanley Cup for the first time. We hollered and cheered, every bit as elated as the rest of the crowd. We were part of the whole thing—voices celebrating together, white voices, black voices, brown voices. I knew I was Palestinian, but I was too young to understand racism. I had this innocent idea that people's skin came in different colours, depending on where they were from, that they went to different sorts of churches, and that this was perfectly normal.

That fall, I put on sunglasses and a new Edmonton Oilers cap as I left to catch the bus to Glengarry Elementary, which had an Arabic immersion program. My father sold accessories like these at his store, so we had some around the house, and I figured that wearing shades and an Oilers cap would make me look more like the white Canadian kid I desperately wanted to become. But I never got out the door.

"Mowafa, where do you think you're going? Come back here, *now!*" My mother was always terrified that I would assimilate into Canadian culture and lose awareness of my Palestinian heritage—as if we could ever be *allowed* to forget that!—and she saw every attempt I made to fit in as a deliberate act of rebellion. Her tone when she spoke ripped through me, and I ran. She chased me down the hallway, spanked me, and ripped off the

Oilers hat with a strength I'd never seen before. Then she broke the sunglasses into pieces. I walked to school crying, wishing I belonged to some other family.

This was the early 1980s, when the idea of an Islamic awakening, or *sahwa,* was flourishing throughout the Arab world. My mother became increasingly aware of traditional Muslim values and of building a sense of Islamic community. Among the things she did for the community was to initiate the idea for a pre-school at Al-Rashid Mosque. She was elected president of the pre-school, an achievement she is very proud of even if people do not recognize her accomplishment today. Along with many other women in Edmonton's Muslim community, my mother began wearing the hijab to identify herself publicly with our religion. To me, it felt like she and others were hammering away to build a walled compound—trying to keep us safe at all costs.

As a kid, I resented this reaffirmation of our Islamic heritage. All it meant was that I would stand out, and not in a way I wanted. At least my father wasn't as adamant about traditional Muslim values. At the time, he was pretty lax when it came to performing religious duties, and he didn't see much reason to import Muslim values into everyday life.

Then, in 1985, everything changed. We were at the mosque one evening when my father's close friend, Uncle Youssef, and several other people suddenly came running in. It was Uncle Youssef who broke the news to my father. Someone had broken into the warehouse and had stolen the container truck with his inventory in it. They had taken what they wanted, then set fire to the truck, destroying the remainder of the stock worth hundreds of thousands of dollars in sales revenue. At first, my father was speechless, and then he began to weep. It was the first time I had ever seen him cry. He had started out as a worker in a cement factory when he arrived, then worked as a travelling salesman.

It had taken him years to build up his own business, and the whole family was proud of his success. When I visited his store filled with giftware and toys, I felt like it belonged to me too.

My father did not have any insurance coverage, so he lost a significant amount of money in the fire, and he had neither the money to pay back investors nor the will to begin again. For him, losing his business was like losing his sense of purpose—it was like being uprooted, yet again. I remember him bursting out in frustration one evening, saying "Screw this—I'm going home." He handed over what remained of the business to Uncle Adnan and asked him to deal with his creditors while he prepared to move to Jordan. In retrospect, I think my dad needed to escape from what felt like a hostile country to him, a place where he was somehow condemned to failure. He needed the comfort of the familiar.

My mother was not enthusiastic about the idea of moving, but she felt it was her duty to follow her husband and support him in times of trouble. For her, moving to the Middle East meant she had to start over again, which caused my mother a great deal of stress about the quality of health care, education, and finances.

To compound her hesitation, she worried about being isolated. In Edmonton, she had made friends to whom she could talk to about her marital problems, but she did not have anyone like that in Jordan. Her brothers and sisters lived in Sweden, and she was not close to her Jordanian cousins. Living in Jordan would make her more dependent on my father and his family.

As for us children, we were all still too young to understand these complications. All I knew was that we were packing up and moving back to Jordan.

For my father, Jordan may have been "home," but Amman was foreign to me—a rougher place, noisy and crowded. We had little money left after the loss of the business and the cost of relocation, and we lived in a modest two-bedroom apartment. My siblings and I—all five of us—slept on the floor in one bedroom, while my parents slept in the other room. Even so, my parents found the money to send us to private schools because they valued education. The schools were strict. I remember how, one day, I was hit with a wooden ruler in front of the class for not doing my homework. When my father found out, he was enraged. He came straight to the school and stormed up to the teacher, dragging me with him. "My son is Canadian," he shouted. "Don't ever do that to him again!" I felt embarrassed and confused. In Canada, I didn't fit because I was Palestinian. Now, in Jordan, I didn't fit because I was Canadian—although apparently this entitled me to privileged treatment. In our final year in Jordan, my father was unable to afford the private school fees, so instead we went to the United Nations Relief and Works Agency school.

Once we were back in Jordan, my father managed to start a new business, Mata'aam wa Halawiyat Househ, the Househ Restaurant and Bakery, in the Jabal al-Nuzha neighbourhood of Amman, not too far from the El-Hussein camp. I could sense that it gave him real satisfaction to be able to provide food for people, even if they were expected to pay for it. He did well for a time, and he insisted on having our apartment furnished in a Canadian way, which was quite unlike the furnishings in the apartments that many of our Middle Eastern neighbours had. The thick carpets and soft leather couches made me feel like I was back in Edmonton. He also installed a *hamam Franji*, a Western-style toilet, so that we could sit rather than squat. His confidence returned. He was back in Jordan and able to surround his family with comforts that, as a child, he couldn't even imagine in the refugee camp.

One day, a young boy passed by my father's restaurant. It was snowing, and he was walking barefoot, wearing only pants and a thin shirt. He made his way along the street, begging for help from those going into and out of the shops. My dad spotted him and shouted into the street, "Where are you who claim to be religious, letting this boy freeze to death?" My father brought him into the restaurant and fed him. He went out bought him two pairs of shoes, pants, shirts, a jacket, and socks. He also gave him some money before he let the boy go. I sometimes wonder what happened to that boy, who was about my age. For my father, faith was something one lived. He taught me to be suspicious of pious words that were not backed up by actions.

Despite its initial success, my father's restaurant ultimately failed as a result of theft and my father's poor financial management. Our deteriorating financial situation put a lot of stress on my parents' relationship. They argued a lot. My father didn't want to return to Canada for fear of being seen as a failure by his Canadian relatives, but my mother put her foot down. He could stay behind if he wanted, she said, but she was leaving, along with the children. She had no money of her own, so she asked her brother Adnan, who had immigrated to Canada shortly before my parents came over and owed my father some money, to buy the airline tickets for her, even though they were not particularly close. I was too young to understand all of what was going on between my parents, but I knew they were angry and unhappy and that returning to the Middle East had not been such a good thing for them financially, or for their marriage. In the end, they decided that my mother and my siblings would return to Canada, but that I would stay with my dad in Amman while he sold his restaurant and found a buyer for our apartment. Everyone else left, leaving me lonely and forlorn. I missed my mother, and I wanted to be with the rest of the family, not stuck in Amman, with only my father for company.

A few months later, I was sent back to Canada with my uncles, Saleh and Riyadh, while my father waited for the money from the sale of the apartment. Because Uncle Saleh couldn't speak English, I was told to act as his interpreter. During my time in Jordan, I had forgotten a lot of my English and on the flight home I mistakenly told Uncle Saleh to put salt in his coffee because I couldn't read the label on the container and guessed the word. An already stressful trip instantly became worse. According to my passport, we landed in New York on September 11, 1988. During our stopover, I struggled to remember how to order a cheeseburger. I was terrified that I would end up with the wrong thing.

When we finally arrived in Edmonton, my mother hugged me for a long time. She was as relieved as I was that we were together again. She and my brothers and sisters were renting a three-bedroom townhouse in northwest Edmonton, in an area called Castle Downs. I'd been back for two months before my father returned and rejoined Uncle Faisal at the giftware business. I don't remember him talking much about Jordan after that. It was as if the whole thing had never happened, but the fault lines that had appeared in my parents' relationship in Jordan remained. It did not help that they both avoided any conversation about their situation. Living on her own had also changed my mother, and that compounded the situation even more. We stayed in the Castle Downs house for about a year until my father and was able to purchase a house for us to live in. Even so, it was difficult for my father to re-establish himself financially in Canada.

I had completed Grades 3, 4, and 5 in Jordan, so in the fall of the year we returned to Canada, I entered Grade 6 at Lorelei Elementary School. It was a strange experience because although I quickly regained my understanding of English, I was afraid people would laugh at me if I spoke the language. As a result of my hesitancy to speak English, I was put in an ESL class, but it felt weird to be relearning a language I had spoken fluently before our sojourn to Jordan. However, I was very motivated to relearn English and picked it up again in no time at all.

WEST

الغرب

7

Uprisings

I had just turned ten, and I was still living in Jordan, when an uprising began in the Jabalia refugee camp in Gaza after an Israeli Army truck had ploughed into a line of cars waiting at a checkpoint, killing four Palestinians. Many thousands of Palestinians had been killed by Israeli forces over the years, but this incident was the spark in the tinder box.

In Gaza, in the West Bank, and in East Jerusalem, Palestinians rose to protest the Israeli military occupation. For the most part, the protesters were unarmed civilians. They erected barricades; they took part in mass demonstrations and general strikes; they boycotted Israeli products; they refused to pay taxes; they scribbled graffiti on walls. Although they sometimes fought back against Israeli troops by throwing stones or Molotov cocktails, the UNLP (the Unified National Leadership of the Uprising) deliberately discouraged the use of firearms in favour of civil disobedience.

Seldom guilty of underreacting, Israel deployed some seventy thousand soldiers to quell these acts of resistance. Israeli forces began by using live ammunition, but as the number of civilian deaths rose and the United Nations Security Council condemned

Israeli policy, the soldiers were equipped instead with clubs, supplemented by rubber-coated metal bullets and plastic bullets. By the end of the first year of the uprising, 332 Palestinians were dead. According to Wendy Pearlman in her book, *Violence, Nonviolence, and the Palestinian National Movement,* Israeli casualties stood at twelve.

This uprising came to be known as the First Intifada. It began in December 1987 and lasted for six years.

When I was in Grade 7, one of my friends, Nuno, came to my house hoping to play video games—*Super Mario, Blades of Steel, Duck Hunt.* We both loved the hollow sound of the spring clicking inside the orange and grey Nintendo gun as we fired at targets. He waited outside while I asked my mother for permission to invite him in.

"Is he Muslim?" she asked. He wasn't.

"Is he Arabic?" Again I had to say no.

"Then I don't want you playing with him. He doesn't belong to our religion and culture." My mother knew that my dad was always worried we would integrate and forget our heritage and religion if he didn't monitor our friendships. That never happened, and Nuno and I are friends to this day.

I glared at her. I couldn't see what religion and culture had to do with playing Nintendo, but I knew it was hopeless to argue with her. I went back outside and said, "Not today, Nuno." I was embarrassed. I was back in Canada, trying again to be normal. But my mother was making this impossible. It was as if she was loved the idea of being an outsider.

If there had been an all-Muslim school in Edmonton, I would have been in it. But there wasn't, so my parents—mostly my mother—found ways to make up for it. On weekends, we would spend all our free time at the Al-Rashid Mosque or go to visit other Muslim families. The only parties I was allowed to attend were those organized by the mosque or by the Canadian Arab Friendship Association. I had the feeling that my mom thought I would end up in some kind of Hell for Children if I went to a "real" party, the kind that Canadian kids had. But then my mother never had any non-Muslim friends either. *So what did you come back to Canada for?* I wanted to ask her. *Aren't we all supposed to be multicultural?*

I remember being sent to a retreat for youth organized by the Al-Rashid Mosque when I was in my early teens. I resented the experience, and, like a typical teenager, I held my mother responsible for my misfortune. When I got back from the camp, I tried to get back at my mother for sending me. If she wanted me to be more Muslim, I reasoned, I'd give her what she wanted. I started eating with my hands, the way I'd seen some other Muslim friends do. My efforts were met with a curt, "Stop eating with your hands."

"That's what they taught me at the retreat," I'd reply. And so it would continue. The bickering seldom stopped, and although we are best of friends now, I cannot recall many conversations with my mother from that time in my life that did not involve fighting. My selfishness made me overlook the many things she did for us, like taking us to piano or swimming lessons, or taking us to the library or taekwondo. At the time, I just resented her and her inability to adjust to a Canadian way of life, as I saw it.

It didn't help that my name, properly transliterated from Arabic, is spelled Mowafaq. The kids loved it. "Mo-fuck you!" they would yell in the schoolyard to embarrass me. So, in Grade 7, while I was still at Killarney Junior High, I changed my name to Moe. A lot of my friends did the same thing—Chadi became Chad; Muhammad called himself Mike; Saeed became Sid. But it didn't really help. An Arab by any other name is still an Arab.

In Grade 8, after the start of the First Gulf War in August 1990, my Arab friends and I got called names like "Camel jockey!" or "Paki!" The antagonism made us feel alienated and rebellious—at home I wasn't Muslim enough and at school I was not allowed to forget I was a Muslim.

I was a moody kid, at once self-conscious about my ethnic background and yet ready to defend it at the drop of a hat. Part of me was desperate to fit in, and part of me was angry that I wasn't allowed to—not by my mother and not by white kids at school. Like most adolescents, I was also keenly sensitive to differences in social and economic status, and this was another source of pain. My family was managing to get by, but it wasn't like the old days before my father lost his business in the fire. At that age, though, I had little understanding of household finances. Nor did I care.

To me, my mother just seemed clueless. She would buy me clothes at the BiWay store—a betrayal that made me want to disappear. Nothing was more humiliating than the BiWay brand logo. We were on the wrong side of the line between those who didn't have to shop at discount warehouses that reeked of sweatshop adhesives and those who did. At school, everyone made fun of people who bought anything other than chocolate bars and gum at BiWay. When I saw the store bags come home, I wanted to explode. I would beg my mother not to go there, but she didn't understand.

We did not have a nice car. We had an old Pontiac, a burgundy station wagon. I didn't want my friends to see it, so I would get my mom to drop me off three or four blocks from the school. My excuse was always the same: "I just feel like walking." I didn't know it at the time, but I was doing the same thing my father had done back in the refugee camp—trying to keep up false appearances to avoid feeling ashamed.

≪ · ≫

As I struggled with my identity in Canada, trying to sort through warring emotions that pulled me in two directions, the Intifada continued in the occupied territories. My father and Uncle Faisal followed the resistance movement closely, and my parents and other family members often talked about it. Some were very worried, especially my mother, who had a sister living in a camp in Mukhayyam Balata, which was located adjacent to Nablus in the occupied West Bank. Many of the casualties were ordinary women and children attempting to defend their neighbourhoods. Schools were closed. Utilities were cut off. Homes were demolished. People were arrested and jailed.

Accounts of the Intifada are full of statistics. In sufficient quantity, numbers work like anesthetic, allowing us to blot out our feelings. But a few stand out for me. During the first two years of the Intifada, an estimated 23,600 to 29,900 Palestinian children required medical treatment for injuries sustained in beatings. Arthur Neslen points out *In Your Eyes a Sandstorm: Ways of Being Palestinian* that a third of these children were under ten years old—younger than I was when it started. In those two years, children died at an average of one every five days. Some were victims of tear gas; others died from beatings, or from gunshot wounds, or from burns. Of these children, 35 percent were under eleven; 19 percent were less than a year old.

In 1993, when I was nearly sixteen, Israel and the PLO signed the first Oslo Accord, thus marking an end to the uprising. By then, upwards of twelve hundred Palestinians—the majority of them unarmed civilians—had been killed by Israeli forces since the Intifada began. News images of Israeli soldiers viciously clubbing Palestinian youth had at one point evoked a certain sympathy in the West for our struggle in Gaza and the West Bank, but by 1993 this compassion had largely evaporated. In Edmonton, as elsewhere, the mood had turned against Palestine.

8

Fighting Back

I remember how, when I was a little kid, I loved to watch morning cartoons. In one of them—I forget which—a Middle Eastern sheik figure sometimes appeared, with his flowing robes and turban. He was always up to no good—sometimes lecherous, sometimes conniving, always greedy. At the time, I did not see the stereotype that was being portrayed—I just thought he was funny. As I grew older, I became increasingly aware of being stereotyped myself, but it never seemed to occur to me that I was just as ready to stereotype other children.

The abuse I endured at Killarney Junior High had made me very unhappy, and so my parents decided it was best to change schools in Grade 8. Dickinsfield Junior High had a substantial minority of Muslim students who came from the large Arab Canadian community in the area. The reason for this larger Arab presence in the area was, in part, because many refugees were allocated government housing in the Castle Downs or Dickinsfield neighbourhoods when they arrived. Other immigrants followed them there to be closer to communities in which they felt more welcome. I used the change of school to change my image, as I wanted to be seen as cool rather than as a loser.

Besides, my best friend Bashar attended Dickinsfield, as did my cousins.

However, the First Gulf War broke out shortly before the start of the new school year, and that brought a new set of problems that pulled me right back into the cycle I had tried escape by coming to Dickinsfield. One morning, not too long after the school year started, I saw a white student taping a picture of Saddam Hussein to the door of his locker. Anti-Saddam sentiments were running high in Canada, and the poster was intended to be a target that other students could spit and throw things at as they shouted things like "Dirty Arab." Others shouted, "I hope they kill that Paki!" I didn't know a whole lot about Saddam Hussein, but I knew he wasn't from Pakistan. I also knew that I wasn't an Iraqi. That didn't seem to matter, though, and it bothered me a lot. If I ever confused Canadians with Americans, I'd be in trouble—so how come white people couldn't keep their Arabs straight?

Life at school was hard. If we had had support from the adults at school, things might have been different, but the teachers, principals, and community were openly racist towards us. I do not remember having any teachers in Dickinsfield or later at M.E. Lazerte who was a person of colour. This racism led me to develop an animosity that bordered on hatred for white people in positions of power. We were the real outsiders; we were the unwanted. I was at a rebellious age, and in this atmosphere of hatred spurred by the Gulf War, the only outlet that some of the Arab kids could find was to engage in gang culture. The Black, Italian, and Chinese students all had their groups, and so Arab kids gravitated towards each other in the same way.

Outside of school, things were much the same. Wherever I went, I could hear people talking, saying things like, "Saddam Hussein! Such an awful man, such a tyrant, such a murderer!" That was all I heard on the news and all around me in Edmonton.

Stories circulated about how he and his sons tortured people for fun. How he was like an Arab Hitler and how Canadians were proud that their country was sending troops to help defeat him. It seemed like a lopsided encounter to me—this huge coalition, led by the United States, heading into the desert to rid the world of one evil dictator.

At home, whenever family and friends visited, there would be long discussions of the Gulf War. As I understood it, Iraq claimed that Kuwait was part of its own territory—that the British had created an artificial country—and it was also accusing Kuwait of siphoning off oil from Iraqi oil fields. The United States was no friend of Iraq, and it wanted to prevent oil-rich Kuwait from falling under Iraqi control. It seemed to me even then that the fight wasn't really about Saddam Hussein: it was about oil.

My parents and their friends were concerned about the long-term ramifications of the war, and the implications it would have for Palestinians. Over the years, the PLO had received support from both Iraq and Kuwait, and Yasser Arafat had learned to balance his Palestinian interests and broader regional interests well. Now, however, the region was divided, and Arafat found himself in a difficult position. Iraq was insisting on a resolution of the "Palestinian problem" as a precondition to its withdrawal from Kuwait, while Kuwait supported Western military intervention. If he supported military intervention, he'd lose the support of Iraq, but if he didn't, he'd lose the support of Kuwait. To make Arafat's dilemma even more complicated, Kuwait was home to some four hundred thousand Palestinian refugees and siding with Iraq could affect Kuwait's attitude towards them. Arafat was opposed to Western intervention in what he viewed as an Arab crisis, and in the end he decided to throw his lot in with Iraq. Kuwait publicly condemned the PLO for opposing Western military intervention.

Many of the Muslim adults I overheard in our home approved of Saddam Hussein's strategy. I would hear things like, "He may be a brutal dictator, but at least he has the guts to stand up to Israel." But some worried that if it came to military action, Iraq would surely be defeated by the US-led coalition. Then what would become of the Palestinian population in Kuwait, especially now that the country had turned against the PLO?

The imam of the Al-Rashid Mosque, Youssef Chebli, was among those who refused to portray Saddam Hussein as wholly evil. Although he was critical of Iraq's invasion of Kuwait, he openly praised Hussein for his continued support of the Palestinian cause. Chebli was also an outspoken critic of Western militarism. As he saw it, military action against Iraq would inevitably put civilian lives at risk. When the assault on Iraq finally began in mid-January 1991, Chebli publicly castigated Canada for its role in what he called the "satanic coalition." The local press had a field day. "Local Muslim Cleric Sees Saddam as God's Agent" the *Edmonton Journal* announced; "Muslim Backs 'Hero' Saddam" screamed the *Edmonton Sun*. Suddenly, our imam was a Saddam-lover. He was also the recipient of death threats, and it was not long before the Canadian Security Intelligence Service paid him a visit.

The local Muslim community was divided over Chebli. Some of my parents' friends admired his willingness to dissent from mainstream opinion and to present another side of the story, while others were embarrassed by his outspokenness and attempted to distance themselves from his views. Yet others were angry. They argued that he was too antagonistic and blamed him for inviting attacks on the city's Muslim residents, as well as for the vandalism at the mosque. Some seemed uncertain about how they felt.

For my part, I always had a lot of respect and admiration for Imam Chebli. When my parents were going through their divorce, he spent many nights at our house trying to help them reconcile. He was always generous. But, regardless of whether Chebli was kind to me and my family, or whether his remarks made matters worse for Palestinians, the fact remains that what was happening in Edmonton was happening all across the country.

In the end, no Canadians died fighting in the Gulf War. The victims were right here in Canada—ordinary people who happened to be Muslim and/or Arab. Or who looked like they might be. On the streets, Arab teens were getting jumped by white gangs, and women wearing hijabs were harassed or sometimes outright assaulted. Mosques were being desecrated, Muslim homes and businesses were being vandalized, and imams were receiving hate mail. Even Sikhs were getting called "Lebs" or "dirty Arabs." It was as if the war had tapped into a wellspring of racism, giving people permission to let loose.

I was too young to analyze the situation fully and to understand why "us" needs a "them." But I did understand what it felt like to be insulted and shoved and why my father was worried about letting my mother go out alone. Watching students at my school spit on a picture of Saddam Hussein, I felt like they were doing it to me.

My parents began spending more time at the mosque, and so did other families we knew. People felt isolated, unwanted, angry, frightened, confused, and often bitter. They needed a place to cling together, to talk about what was happening and to support one another. The mosque offered such a space. Even my father started to attend the Friday sermons and the weekday evening lectures. Before the Gulf War, the focus at the mosque was mostly spiritual; now it was political.

Although Iraq invaded Kuwait on 2 August 1990, fighting between Iraq and the Western coalitions forces did not start until January 1991. The intervening time was spent preparing for the war and consolidating support in the West. During that time, a couple of Arab students from Dickinsfield Junior High were beaten up by a group of white students while they were on their way home from school. At that time, I was one of the more outspoken students at the school, and many of my peers looked to me as a leader. Their bruises didn't prevent these kids from walking or talking, and they came and told me what had happened. Although they were more scared than hurt, I could feel things changing.

I was angry about the wave of anti-Muslim sentiment that the invasion had unleashed, and I reacted by asserting my Arab and Islamic identity. At school, as a symbol of rebellion, I started to wear the Palestinian keffiyeh, the scarf that Yasser Arafat always wore. Somewhere in all of this was a desire to show that "Arab is cool." I started to attend events at the mosque more often with my family. I even requested that the school allocate a space to students for the weekly Friday prayer. To my surprise, my requested was granted. So there I was, fronting like some thirteen-year-old imam, giving Friday sermons to my fellow students. I wasn't even sure how to perform the Friday prayer ritual, but I did it anyway, recycling lectures I heard at the mosque.

Around the same time as these world events were unfolding and I began to retreat into myself in an effort to cope, some of my friends and I started hanging out at the Canadian Arab Friendship Association, which was located in the Dickinsfield Mall, just a few blocks away from the school on 144 Avenue. CAFA was established in 1965 by several members of the Arab community who wanted to ensure that their cultural heritage would be preserved for their children. The association also worked to promote an appreciation of Arab traditions in the broader community. One of the people who volunteered at CAFA was Uncle Yazan, who became the father figure I needed at the time. Uncle Yazan is not related to me, but he treated me like a son, and I respected him as though he were family, so I called him Uncle. Uncle Yazan became my mentor and taught me more about Arabic culture and history than anyone had done up to that point in my life.

I'd first met Uncle Yazan before I started going to CAFA, and I confess I started going there mostly to be with him. We met when I got into a fight with a Turkish boy named Baha. Baha and I were going at each other outside the Happy Pop store at the Dickinsfield Mall when the police showed up. Baha fled, and I ran into the Burger Baron restaurant, further down the mall. I had heard that an Arab man called Yazan owned the store and thought I might be safe there. Even though I didn't know him, I trusted him based on the things I'd heard about him. Uncle Yazan hid me in the restaurant storage room. When the cops came into the Burger Baron to ask questions, Uncle Yazan told them, "It was nothing—just a couple of young kids having a fight." The police asked for names, but Yazan said he couldn't give them any.

After they left, Yazan called people he knew and tracked down Baha. He made him come to the store and then sat the two of us down to resolve the problem. I hadn't realized that Baha was Muslim—he looked more European than Arab. We made our peace, and I went home, feeling rather remorseful. It was that day that Uncle Yazan took me under his wing. "Come and see me," he said. "Every week if you can." And I did.

By Grade 11, we had built a close friendship and he used to tease me when he saw me come through the doors at CAFA, by call me "Mr. Arafat" because I wore a keffiyeh, just like Yasser Arafat did.

Maybe a month after my fight with Baha, I was at the Northgate Transit Centre near the Northgate Mall with my pal Bashar and another friend, Chadi, who was older than we were. They were cool, good-looking guys, smart guys—but also guys who wouldn't back down from a street fight. Chadi was in a bad mood that day because he had just broken up with his girlfriend and needed someone to blame. "Let's pick a fight," he said.

Bashar objected, but I wanted to impress Chadi. I did not want to do it, but I was desperate to belong and besides, I'd been taught to respect my elders—and Chadi was older than I was. As a young Arab boy growing up in northeast Edmonton, which had a reputation for being a tough area, I understood instinctively that people did not mess with the tough guys. I hoped that getting into a fight alongside Chadi I would build my reputation as a tough guy and improve my social standing. So, to prove how tough I was, I looked around for the largest white guy, who happened to be about seventeen and stood three inches taller than me. He looked like a skater—all laid-back in a crowd of white kids who thought they were very cool. I sauntered up to him and said, "Hey buddy, gimme a cigarette." He stared at me. "I don't smoke," he answered. Then I pushed him, and he pushed back.

That was all Chadi needed. He jumped in and started to fight with the guy, who fought back, hard. It was short but violent and resulted in bruises and bloody noses. As the guy climbed onto his bus, he pointed at me and shouted, "You coward! Just you wait—I'll be back!"

I will never forget his words as the bus drove off, "I am coming for you."

A few days later Byron and his friends did come for me. At lunch one day, Bashar and I headed out to the Dickinsfield Mall. We planned to get slushies at the Happy Pop store and play Mortal Kombat in the arcade. As we were on our way, two young Arab kids who were in Grade 7 at Dickinsfield came running up. They told me that some white guys were cruising around, looking for me.

"Let's go back to the school," Bashar said.

"Come on, I have a reputation to protect. I don't back down."

The kids were staring at me, waiting to see what I would do. I'd been stung by being called a coward, and if word got out that I'd run from a fight, that would be it for my image at school. So I took off my jacket and said I would defend myself.

"No!" Bashar shouted. "Go back to school and wait it out!"

I should have listened to Bashar.

Three cars pulled up at the side of the road. About ten white guys got out and started walking towards me. They were older than me, obviously in high school. Bashar was yelling at me, "Run, you idiot!" But I stood my ground, trying to convince myself that I could take it. Suddenly I was surrounded. Some of the boys had sticks, while others were rotating their fists in the air. Out of the middle of the mob came Byron, the guy from the Transit Centre.

"I told you I would come back for you," he said.

I thought they were all going to attack me, but he told them to stay back. The only thing I remember after that was that Bashar and another student, Linda, picked me up off the ground and me walked me to the nursing station at the school, where I was cleaned up. The principal called my father to come and pick me up from school.

News of the beating spread like wildfire in the community. Many of the students at Dickinsfield were angry about what had happened to me. What they heard was that fifty kids, most of them white, had showed up to jump me. I didn't bother to correct their version of the events.

When my father arrived at school, he was furious. He had brought a friend of his, Uncle Youssef Chehimi, with him. I'd been too scared to tell my father about the fight I'd started at the bus terminal, and now the two of them wanted the school to bring criminal charges against the attackers. The principal said that he was deeply sorry about what had happened but because it had happened outside of the school grounds, it was a police matter, and there was nothing he could do. Technically, he was correct: the principal's authority stopped at the boundary of the school grounds. However, he could have offered to speak to the children involved, or he could have set up a program to foster greater understanding. But that was not how things went those days, especially not during the height of anti-Arab sentiment during the Gulf War. Uncle Youssef was a tough guy, like the Joe Pesci character in *Goodfellas*. "Listen to me," he said. "If you don't do it your way, we will do it our way."

When my father and Uncle Youssef left the office, they were fuming. Yet, despite their threatening words, they didn't actually do anything. It would just make things worse, they figured, what with the Gulf War and all. I was scared and regretted my actions. It was only recently, after I was diagnosed with ADHD, that I came to realize how much of my impulsive behaviour as a child may have been the result of that disorder rather than just my troubled family life and my anger at what was happening in the Middle East. My father and Uncle Youssef may have decided to leave matters be, but others were in no mood to do that, and since I was in the middle of the situation, I got pulled into planning the revenge. I simply did not have the courage or maturity to stand up to my friends at the time.

We met at CAFA under the auspices of a youth meeting. Our plan was to collect some sticks to use as weapons and then to gather at Northgate Mall bus terminal after school. From there, we would go together to Bishop O'Leary school, which is where Byron and his friends went to school. I did not want to go. I was hurting emotionally, and I was wrestling with the situation and my role in it. I still do.

By noon, about sixty of us were waiting outside the Bishop O'Leary. Some had walked; others came in cars. Ahmad, an old-school Palestinian, had managed to stuff more than twelve people into his family's minivan. To my embarrassment, my father was there too, standing on the sidewalk outside the school. I could see some kind of metal bar in his hands. I couldn't believe it. What did he think he was doing? My father was never violent. Whether I was embarrassed at the sight of him carrying a metal bar, or at my own presence in the midst of this violence when that was not the way I had been raised, I am not sure. My only course of action, I felt, was to avoid my father. I withdrew to the sidelines, out of view and wracked with guilt at the thought that the events that were unfolding had happened because of me.

I watched my father and the other people who had gathered approach the school. I watched my dad move to the sidelines, but still I was ashamed. I realize now that the only way my father knew how to show solidairty with the injustice that had been visited on his son was to be a bystander. But then I saw only that I had let him down and had forced him to engage in uncharac-teristic violence.

Then a random white guy yelled at my father, "Get out of here before I beat you up, you fucking Paki!"

My father responded by waving the metal rod in his hands defiantly before getting back into his car and moving it to the other side of the street, further down the block. That was when I realized that my mother was with him. I don't know why. The whole thing seemed crazy. Perhaps they were simply scared of what was going to happen and wanted to be there regardless. Or perhaps my father was content to stand by and watch while other people fought for his son. I could not tell. And did my mother want to witness this revenge as well? I remembered her strength when she ripped the Oilers cap off me and smashed my sunglasses and wondered whether she planned to join the fray. I could picture the headlines: "Avenging Arab Mom Unleashes Fury Upon High School Kids."

Byron and his skater friends were nowhere to be seen in the schoolyard, so we headed inside the school to look for him. Still no luck. So we went after anyone we thought looked like a skater or a headbanger—basically, white dude with long hair parted to one side, baggy clothes, and skateboard became a legitimate target. We were an angry mob of youngsters who were determined to frighten anyone who would attack one of our own. After about ten minutes of fighting and mayhem, we ran off before the police showed up.

Looking back, it seems like a sad thing to feel proud of, but I felt proud. I had seen how our community could close ranks in defence of one of our own. Guys I didn't even know had been willing to risk getting beaten up and maybe even arrested, just to deliver a message. It felt like our own Intifada, in the middle of the Gulf War.

9

Wise Mentors, Rough Waters

No matter how hard I tried to fit in at school, I constantly felt rejected. I responded by not wanting to have anything to do with white Anglo-Christian Canada. I wanted to be Palestinian, Arab, and Muslim, even though I did not understand what that really meant. At home, I felt pressure from my parents to hold onto my past and the history and customs of my people. I was an emotional powder keg, and the spark that lit the fuse was the First Gulf War. After 9/11, I remember seeing non-Muslims come to the mosque with flowers. That never happened in 1990.

Furthermore, I struggled with Islam. Not with my faith per se, but with the definition of Islam that my parents saw, which was largely cultural and had little to do with Islam as a religion. Many of my friends and I were unsure of what Islam did and did not allow us to do in a Canadian cultural context. For instance, dating felt foreign—wrong and sinful. We often wondered whether we might end up burning in hell for doing things that non-Muslim kids did. A lot of our frustration came out through fighting. Looking back, I can see that it was a constant battle for immigrant parents to try to raise their kids within their culture but also within the reality of Canadian norms. Those parents who had endured *ghurba* (exile) and all that went with it now had to battle with their kids, who faced their own inherited displacement.

After the Byron incident and our reprisal, I felt I had some kind of stupid tough guy image to maintain. It became cool to be bad and I enjoyed the attention, even though I did not feel good about what I was doing. For the first time, I felt accepted and felt like I belonged. Younger kids at the school looked up to me, so I continued to behave in ways I now regret.

Our attack at O'Leary High sparked fears that things would get worse, and that the cycle of violence would continue. Community police officers and Arab community leaders organized a large meeting at O'Leary to call for a truce. We were sitting on one side of the hall, and Byron and the other skaters were on the other side, with the police and Uncle Yazan in the middle. The police officer started to talk: "We want to end this fight here and now because if you guys don't, it will get worse, and we will have to lay charges." I remember my friend Majid saying to Byron, "You are lucky. If I had found you that day, I would have smashed your face in."

Another fight almost broke out, but Uncle Yazan, whom we all looked up to and respected, intervened. His baritone voiced grabbed our attention. "Sit down and don't make any more wise-ass comments like that," he said.

At the end of the session, Byron and I apologized and shook hands. I was embarrassed about my part, an embarrassment I still feel today. I wish I could say it was all over, and that I stopped getting into fights, but it wasn't. I continued to get into scraps, with my own people too. One afternoon in Home Economics class, Bashar and I were talking about the Gulf War and got into an argument over who would come out victorious, Saddam or the United States. Bashar felt, as I and many others in the community did, that a defeat for Saddam was a defeat for Palestinians. But to egg me on, he said, "America is going to win and destroy Saddam."

We started punching each other in the middle of the class. This led to another suspension.

We were right, after all. Saddam lost the war, and the Palestinians in Kuwait lost their refuge. Palestinians had arrived in Kuwait in three different waves—in 1948, 1967, and 1975. By 1990, Kuwait, a country of only about two million, was full of Palestinian workers. The national demographics were threatened, and the expulsion began. In 1991, after Kuwait's liberation from Iraqi invasion, 300,000 Palestinian were expelled. Things have come full circle since then. During the uprisings of 2021, Kuwait has taken one of the most patriotic stands with the Palestinian people and has imposed a fine and a prison sentence of ten years for any Kuwaiti who actively supports Israel.

At the time of the Gulf War, I was a teenager, and I knew about the struggles my grandfather, my parents, and my family had endured simply to survive and resist oppression. With the expulsions happening in Kuwait, it seemed as though my father and uncles were reliving their own exile. Every time something like this happened, my father and my uncles felt like it was another strike at our people. It seemed like those who left during the seven-month occupation would never return to Kuwait. Kuwaiti officials suggested that the Palestinians could move to Jordan. It was always the same dilemma: *Where do we go, where do we belong?* It is something I struggle with to this day, this search for a place to call home and put down roots.

For as far back as I could remember, my parents had struggled with their marriage and with their relationship to us children. My father was always on the road as a travelling salesman, so we barely saw him or bonded with him. I know he has a good heart and is very, very generous, and very forgiving. I also know that he enjoyed hanging out with his friends more than with his family. I never remember him taking us on a vacation or taking me with him on his sales trips. I used to beg him to take me with him while he travelled, but he never did. My mom is a kind, forgiving, and loving person who has never harmed anyone. She avoids confrontation wherever possible and is always ready to help others. She is also conservative and very spiritual and religious. Growing up, we watched the combination of their personalities build into a disaster.

By 1992, the cracks in my parents' relationship had become chasms and my own outbursts in and out of school did not help to settle our family's lives. To escape the chaos of life in Edmonton and to be away from my father, my mother decided to move to Montréal for a year to be near her sister. She took me and my bothers with her, hoping that removing us from that environment would help settle us. I was fifteen at the time. We flew to Toronto and planned to take the train to Montréal the next day. We wandered with our suitcases around the cavernous lobby of the Royal York Hotel next to Union Station. My mom could not afford the $300 for a room, and we planned to wait overnight in the hotel lobby. My brothers and sister were getting restless. They were exhausted from the flight and needed to rest.

We had been sitting on the couches, surrounded by our bags, for about two hours when a white woman who worked at the hotel approached my mom. "Are you okay?" she asked.

"Yes, we are fine," my mom replied. "We are waiting for the train. We will be leaving in the morning."

The woman asked my mom if she was a single mother. My mom nodded, wondering why she would ask such a strange question.

The woman then asked if she could speak to my mother in private. My mom agreed and they walked to the woman's office, which was near the lobby of the hotel. I watched through the doorway as the lady sat behind her office desk at a computer terminal, with my mother sitting on opposite side. I could not hear what she was saying and was too young to read her body language. All I remember is that my mother was crying when she left the office. I wondered what the woman had said that had made my mother cry. Then I saw two sets of keys in her hands and realized they were tears of happiness. The woman had given us two free rooms for the six of us!

Then I, too, wanted to cry, and I felt my body fill with hope that God was with her and was helping us. How good it felt, as the oldest, to put one of those sets of keys into the door lock of a hotel room. Once inside, it felt like we had stepped into a dream with fancy décor and pillows everywhere. We kids jumped on the beds and eventually fell asleep to rest for the next leg of our journey. We even received a courtesy wake-up call the next morning, and staff to help us with our baggage. I wish to this day that I could find that woman to thank her for what she did for my mother, and to tell her that my mother has paid that gift forward in her own way, too.

My mother has given back that generosity many times over. To this day, my mother helps people. I remember in my second year at university I went to visit her in Richmond, BC, where she had rented a small basement suite. One night, she asked me and my brother Belal to sleep on the couch so that she could let an abused woman who needed shelter stay in our room. I may have been a troubled youth, but I have learned from her, and I try to live by similar values.

The train ride to Montréal seemed to go by very quickly after the long flight and a good night's rest. When we arrived, my aunt and uncle picked us up at the train station. Having no place of our own, we stayed with them for a couple of weeks. As the house was very cramped, I decided to ride the bus and look for a place to live. One day, I stumbled on a three-bedroom apartment for $700 a month in Saint-Laurent, near the Côte-Vertu subway stop. It was in an area with a high concentration of Arabs, called Al-Mukhayyam, which means "the refugee camp." I told my mom about it when I got home, and she came to look at it with me the next day. She signed the lease right away. She then arranged for the boxes containing our possessions to be shipped from Edmonton. When the boxes arrived, they filled the new space with a mountain of cardboard that gradually disappeared as we unpacked and restarted our lives.

I started Grade 10 at Émile Legault Secondary, where the students came from a variety of backgrounds, and the student body included Arabs, Muslims, Christians, and Lebanese. As an expression of my style and identity, I wore my black and white Palestinian keffiyeh to school.

One day, I was approached by three guys. They pushed me against my locker and spoke loudly in French, which I struggled to understand. Then they switched to Arabic. They wanted me to take off my keffiyeh, and they were quite blunt about it—that much was clear regardless of the language they chose to speak. I hated being outnumbered like this. I did not comply, but fortunately a mutual friend turned up at that moment to stick up for me, and nothing more serious happened to me.

One of our neighbours, a Lebanese girl named Lilian, and I had become friends soon after we had moved into the apartment in Al-Mukhayyam. I would walk home with her after school every day and I learned later that the guys who had roughed me up were Lebanese Christians, and did not like Palestinians, especially not Palestinian Muslim boys, hanging around Lilian.

Later that year, I was getting a caricature drawn of myself at the harbourfront. I was staring at it intently, trying to decide if it really looked like me, and whether the artist had captured the "real me" under the exaggeration. When I looked up, I saw two guys trying to pick up girls. I knew they were Lebanese, but they were wearing necklace chains with the Star of David on them. Curious, I asked if they were Jewish.

They laughed and said, "No, we are Christian Lebanese—but more girls talk to us when we say we are Jewish."

I thought of my own attempts at disguising my identity. I would sometimes say that I was Spanish, and some people thought so anyway, because of how similar Househ and José sound. Sometimes, I realized then, it was simply too much trouble being Arab, or Palestinian, regardless of whether you were Muslim or Christian. And I thought again of the boys who had roughed me up, wondering why Arabs could not simply let other Arabs be.

The year in Montréal sped by and I was just settling in nicely when my mother announced that we were returning to Edmonton. My father had come to Montréal to visit and, I realize now, to woo my mother into returning to Edmonton. I remember he made it seem like he had lots of money to spend on things like a rented car. He even went to the local mosque and brought some people over to show my mom that he had changed. He told her how he had changed and made promises about how everything would be great. He is a salesman, after all, and knows how to be a showman when he needs to be. My mom was reluctant, but she genuinely loved my father, so we packed up our apartment and moved back to Edmonton.

≪ · ≫

Initially, my mom moved back in with my father. I had grown accustomed to not living under my father's thumb, and it felt awkward to be back under his authority. Soon the old, familiar tensions that had driven us to Montréal returned, and my mom moved out again, taking my siblings with her to Vancouver. I chose to stay in Edmonton and live independently. A year older and much wiser for the insights I had gained while in Montréal, I calmed down after moving out of my father's house again and began spending more time with people like Uncle Yazan at the Canadian Arab Friendship Association. For me, he remains one of the most intelligent and dynamic people in the Arab community in Edmonton. Uncle Yazan is both an idealist and a realist. He believed then, as he still does, that Muslims and Arabs are the best of people and are making a beneficial contribution to Canadian society. When we were growing up, he wanted to show us young people how we could contribute in positive ways. He wanted us to be proud of who we were and to discover the many contributions Arabs have made to the world through the centuries in areas like medicine, ethics, and philosophy. He wanted us to know that we did not need to feel ashamed of being Muslim and to look to those examples of Arabs who contributed to the world, not to the hoodlums we saw on television and in the often rougher, crime-ridden communities of northeast Edmonton. Uncle Yazan always respected the youth. He would stand up and shake our hands when he saw us, and he knew how to talk to us at our level. He was generous, paying for things and never wanting anything in return. But more than that, he taught us to love ourselves and where we came from. He would share snippets of Arabic history with us, including the contributions Arabs had made to the arts and sciences: Ibn Sina (known to the west as Avicenna) in medicine, Ibn Rushd (Averroes) in scientific and religious ethics, or Al-Ghazali (Algazel) in algebra.

UNDER THE NAKBA TREE

He told us that there were twenty-two Arabic countries and over a billion Muslims in the world at that time—in 2015, the Pew Research Center estimated there were close to 1.8 billion Muslims, or 24 percent of the world's population. Just like Uncle Faisal, my honorary uncle, Yazan Haymour, was always available when I needed support.

I went to Uncle Yazan with my personal, and sometimes even trivial, problems. When my parents were splitting up, I lived with my father. One day, I went to visit my mother and noticed she was wearing earrings. It may seem like a small thing, but my dad had a phobia of earrings and objected to anyone wearing them around him. When my mom wore them at home, I knew she was doing it just to antagonize him, and it upset me. I went to Uncle Yazan crying about how my mother wore earrings at home. Uncle Yazan calmed me down and smiled.

"It is okay, Mowafa," he said. "It is a natural reaction to now being set free from your father. It is just a phase, and they will get back together." He was not always right, but he knew how to make me feel better.

As teens, we would tell him, "These girls love us, Uncle Yazan."

"Of course they do, of course they do," he'd reply. "The Arabs are the most handsome people in the world."

He made us believe it. We clung to this belief, especially since we never heard it anywhere else. Like many teenage guys, we thought about girls constantly, even as we were overprotective of our sisters. Uncle Yazan understood how high school students were often thinking about things other than studies and homework and he took our concerns seriously. We all appreciated that.

Failure to keep a family and marriage together represented the defeat of our Palestinian nation, now fragmented as well, and my parents were the only Palestinian couple I knew who were splitting up. I was on edge and didn't entirely understand why.

The hardest question to face in our small community was, "How are your parents doing, Mowafa?" The reality contained in this question, that others knew about the collapse my parents were enduring, hurt as much as the racism I faced every day.

On our return to Edmonton from Montréal, I attended Queen Elizabeth High School, which had a large population of Arab students. The Arabs students took to hanging out in big groups, partly to avoid getting beaten up by racist whites. The fights we got into now were more violent than they had been in junior high at Dickinsfield, and sometimes involved knives and sticks, and we needed to protect ourselves. Yet there was something about being part of a big group that tempted us to abuse our collective power. We could see that some of the students were afraid of us, and we enjoyed watching them treat us with a sort of fake deference. Since many of the Arab students at Queen Elizabeth were of Lebanese descent, other students soon started referring to the group I hung out with collectively as "Lebs."

Many Arab kids took advantage of the newfound reputation we enjoyed as part of the Lebs, and very soon younger Arab kids no longer hung out with us because we were a cultural safety net. Now it was just about status, about feeling powerful. Quite a few Lebs got into the local bar scene, which was pretty violent, and some of them got into crime and drugs. After a while, it became embarrassing to be identified as a Leb because it meant you were a hoodlum. All the same, it gave us a sense of belonging in a school environment that often consciously alienated us.

By the time I was in Grade 11, the Canadian Security Intelligence Service started to take an interest in me. It was Uncle Yazan who told me about this. He said it was because I encouraged some of the younger students, who looked up to me, to wear the Palestinian keffiyeh. I had also given them stick-on temporary tattoos of the Palestinian flag, an idea I'd come up with after watching the Mexican gang movie *Blood In, Blood Out*. He wasn't trying to frighten me, but I was really scared. Ever since the Gulf War, I'd heard about people being targeted and interrogated by the Canadian Security Intelligence Service and the RCMP. The Canadian Arab Federation responded by producing and distributing a series of know-your-rights pamphlets among Arab communities in the city as a precautionary measure. I'd read one titled "When CSIS Calls," and it scared me to think that a powerful organization like CSIS would think to come after a high school student. Did they have a whole file on me? Had they been following me, taking photos, and making notes? Had they tapped our phone? I didn't know, and neither did Uncle Yazan—he just knew that I was being investigated. Knowing that I was under intelligence scrutiny made me feel even more unwelcome.

Someone who added to my sense of alienation was Constable Case Model, a police officer stationed at Queen Elizabeth High School. One day at the police station, a few of us were waiting for the release of our friend Nader, who was being questioned about a fight that had taken place at Northgate Bus Terminal. Constable Case Model saw me. "What are you Lebs doing here? Were you in another fight again? Why don't you find something better to do, like drive a cab or something?"

I had always found it frustrating that people called me a "Leb" despite the fact that I made a point of asserting publicly that I was Palestinian. But Constable Case Model had done more than jus that. He had not only made a racist generalization, but he also implied that we were inferior and had limited potential. I wish I had filed a complaint against him, but I was a sixteen-year-old who didn't yet know you could do these things.

It often seemed as though all white people were against us, but there was one who reached out to our community. While in high school, I met Mr. Dennis Koch through my friend Jihad. As the teacher liaison, Mr. Koch's role at the school had to do with career development and counselling. He didn't seem popular with the other teachers. He was the kind of guy one suspects ended up sitting alone in the teachers' lounge. Dennis Koch was unique. He worked with the Arab community and with CAFA in a way we were not used to and seemed to know and to understand both worlds. He was one of the few white people I can recall from my youth who saw us as human beings. He treated us with respect, was a great listener, and always had memorable advice, like "Working hard is fine, but working smart is better."

Somehow, through Dennis Koch, and through CAFA and its youth group, we found ways to deal with our issues and to work with those few police officers, counsellors, and teachers who seemed to want to help. With their involvement, school violence was reduced significantly, but unfortunately the racist attitudes lingered. There did not seem any way racism could be eliminated without painting everyone white—and even then, some people would still notice the paint and point to the difference.

It was after the Gulf War, when many Arab youth were involved in fights and petty crime, and Mr. Koch, together with Uncle Yazan at CAFA, created a youth club called Harmony in the Halls to combat violence within our school. My friends Chadi, Nidal, Marwan, and I started attending Harmony in the Halls events and even got a Harmony in the Halls award for being peacemakers in the school. It was quite a change from being branded a troublemaker. Slowly, my mind turned from causing trouble to thinking about my future and going to university. I left the rowdy crew behind and began to get my life back into shape, even though some called me and my friends who were also trying to clean up their acts rats for leaving the rebellious life. But we had matured and had decided to focus on something that we considered more important.

10

A Thirst for Knowledge

For years, I hadn't cared much about school, but my interest in education and my determination to succeed academically gradually began to grow. As I engaged more with peers at CAFA and at Harmony in the Halls, I realized that education was the only way for me to escape the sense of confinement that came with not belonging. This is something many first-generation immigrants and their children experience and can understand. When you feel you don't belong, it feels as if you get cut off from opportunities. People are unwilling to engage with you as a friend and an equal. In racialized communities, you sense the prejudice. As a child, I felt cloistered by this lack of engagement and opportunity. One of the emotional aspects of immigration is grief—grief at the loss of a homeland and also grief at the perceived loss of one's culture and language. Immigrants deal with these feelings of loss in similar ways to how people deal with death. There is denial, anger, depression, bargaining, and for most immigrants, eventual acceptance of the change. Everyone works through these stages at their own pace, and as I look back at my life, I can see many of these elements of grief in the trajectory of my own family. Though my father was somewhat indifferent about the value of education at the time, my mom pushed me. Her family valued education—her mother's family were professionals from the city of Yaffa, which is more cosmopolitan than Lydda, my father's birthplace. Along with my mother, it was Uncle Yazan, my mentor, who encouraged me.

I was sixteen when my parents separated, and my mother moved to Vancouver. My brother Omar and I went to live with my father. It was not an easy time. Dad did not take the separation well. His mental health declined and being on the road for long stretches of time for his work made his sense of loneliness worse. After a year of mostly looking after myself, I decided to make the break and live independently. I found a place near the Coliseum Station and was barely scraping by as I worked to finish high school. I wanted to go to university but was worried that the same level of ostracization and alienation that haunted me at school would follow me there. When I was seventeen, some friends who were already in university told me about the Arab Students' Association at the University of Alberta. That convinced me that I would find a support community there, so I applied and got accepted.

The only other option I could foresee at the time was for me to work in the family giftware business, which my father had run for over twenty years with my Uncle Faisal, who taught him the ropes when he left the cement factory. I respected what they had done but had no desire to follow in their footsteps. Uncle Faisal was bitter about the fact that he'd had to put aside his education and career to help support the family in the El-Hussein refugee camp in Amman. I also knew how bitter my father was about not being able to continue his pharmacy work in Canada. I decided the wisest choice would be to pursue a university education.

When I was growing up, very few people in my Arab community went to university. When I was contemplating university, Moe Smiley, a Lebanese Canadian acquaintance, asked me, "Why would you go to university? You can work and make much more money. Think about it—you're seventeen, and if you work for ten years and save a thousand dollars a month, at age twenty-seven you could have $120,000."

It was appealing.

"I really don't care about the money," I replied.

"Are you nuts?" said Moe. "You could have it made, rather than spending a boatload of money to go to school, then have to pay that off, then have to find a job, no guarantees."

Moe didn't understand why I had to go to university, but when I began talking about postsecondary education, many people who had known me through high school began to treat me with respect, although they wondered if this was really me.

I chose to study political science because I had grown up in a politicized environment and thought this would be a good direction for someone with my interest in politics. In the first month of classes, I found myself desperately trying just to understand concepts like socialism, communism, and the Canadian parliamentary system, let alone attempt to discuss them at a complex intellectual level. *This whole thing was a mistake,* I thought.

"You should go into the Faculty of Business," said my close friend Bashar. "What are you doing in arts? You won't make any money."

I listened to Bashar. Even though I'd told Moe Smiley I wasn't interested in money, I changed course and registered for a Bachelor of Commerce.

≪ · ≫

I loved the University of Alberta. It was here, among people who understood my difficulties with fitting in, that my sense of being Arab in the world really began to become defined. Even so, I soon noticed differences in our childhood. Many of the other Arab students had not grown up shopping at BiWay. They were clean-cut and much more stylish and academic than my high school friends from the north side. The perception in Edmonton was that the rougher, more troublesome, and more "cultural" Arabs lived in the north end of the city and that they were unlikely to go on to university.

I didn't know many other Arab Canadians pursuing higher learning, but Statistics Canada had figures that might have shocked people like Constable Case Model: in 2001, 74 percent of Arab Canadians aged fifteen to twenty-four were enrolled in a full-time educational program, compared with 57 percent of all Canadians in that age group. Canadians of Arab origin were twice as likely as other Canadians to have a university degree. In fact, in 2001, 30 percent of Arab Canadians aged fifteen and over had a bachelor's or postgraduate degree—twice the percentage of the overall adult population. Also, the proportion of Arab Canadians holding either a master's degree or doctorate (10 percent of adults) was twice as high as that of all Canadian adults.

These turn-of-the-millennium opportunities available to me in Canada contrasted sharply with the opportunities my father had had when he was growing up. Although even the refugee camps had schools, things got tough after the Six-Day War and the capture of the West Bank, and after the First and Second Intifada. With high birth rates and little land for new buildings and agriculture, overcrowding and rising unemployment became harsh realities for Palestinians. Few college-educated Palestinians in the Middle East could find work related to their degrees.

In some ways, I had it easy in Canada. For one, there was no open war zone. However, I struggled with living alone after I had moved out and my mother had moved with my brothers and sisters to Vancouver. My dad stayed in Edmonton, but he worked out of town for his wholesale business, and I rarely saw him. I felt like a teenage orphan, carrying the awful feeling of family separation with me. This was something I could not solve with fighting. Although divorce is not forbidden in Islam, modern Levantine culture—that is to say, the area covered roughly by Syria, Jordan, Lebanon, Palestine, and parts of Turkey—stigmatizes those who separate and divorce. Since a large portion of the Edmonton Arab community came from those regions, people looked down on our family. I noticed how my family was no longer invited to other peoples' homes, or to weddings. Even members of our own family avoided us. There was nothing I could do about my parents' divorce, but it did not stop me from feeling ashamed. Fortunately, other adults stepped in to support me, like Uncle Faisal and Auntie Khadija, and Uncle Andy (Adnan), a dollar-store pioneer who paid my rent for almost two years while I was at university.

At university, my sense of not belonging began to ease. I still felt lonely at times, but I was also becoming part of a close-knit community. When I worked as a purchasing assistant at Brio Beverages one summer, Umm Marwan, the mother of my co-worker Marwan, would send me food every day with her son. Everyone seemed to want to feed me and keep me going. One night at Thanksgiving, when I had just sat down to watch TV and eat a bit of chicken with Stove Top stuffing, my friend Bashar knocked on the window. He saw me eating alone and started to cry, as if I were in the depths of poverty. "Come on," he sobbed, "you're coming home with me." It was a homemade turkey dinner I will never forget.

A year later, I was living closer to the university with the Fayad brothers, Sami and Talal, from Lac La Biche. We found a place near the university, a few steps away from Grandin Station. Talal and Sami were wonderful people, kind and considerate, and great partners for playing Sega video games with, or for walking all over downtown, or going to the occasional party. They also provided me with a sense of belonging that I had not felt before. The Muslim community in Lac La Biche has roots that go back to the 1940s, and the Fayads were among the early Lebanese settlers there.

I did not think of myself as the most intelligent person in my circle, but I had strong ambition and a drive to succeed and to make something out of myself. I had always pushed out in front, whether starting prayer classes and wearing the keffiyeh in Grade 8 or starting a fight in my high school years. If I had made it this far, I knew, nothing could hold me back from accomplishing whatever I wanted to achieve. I began to get active with the university's Arab Student Association, which worked to organize students on campus and to plan the annual Arab Awareness Week. I became a social convener, organizing events and meetings in my first and second years. By my third year, I was vice-president of the ASA, and in my fourth year, I became the president.

One night in my second year of university, I was helping to organize an alcohol-free dinner and theatre event at a local burger joint called Red Robin, when one of the first-year students turned to me.

"Mowafa, I am so proud of you," she said.

"Why?"

"When I was at school, I heard so many bad things about you getting into trouble. But you have proved all those people wrong, and I just wanted to let you know that."

Her remarks caught me off guard. I had worked hard to become a better person, but no one had told me before that they had noticed the changes in me. It felt good to hear her say such things about me.

In high school, I'd occasionally imagined myself becoming a police officer, despite my troubles with the law at that time. I was tall, strong, and quick to learn. It could be a secure job. Perhaps it was simply a reaction to my experiences with Constable Case Model that had made me want to change the culture of the organization from within, but in the end, I decided to go to university instead. One person in our community did join the police force, and few people I knew respected him. In the northside Edmonton community at the time, police were seen as aggressive, hostile, and racist. While I do think attitudes have changed and that it is more acceptable for members of the Arab community to join the police, at the time, he was treated with suspicion as a sell-out. "I'm just doing my job," he would say when people confronted him. This officer was a friend of my cousin Nedal and we visited him once at his house. He struck me as a very decent person. He was very humble and loved being a police officer. He saw his career as an opportunity to do something good, but I had the feeling he was usually alone.

Edmonton is a small city, and when I was studying at the University of Alberta, I ran into a spectre from my past in the washroom in HUB Mall one day. It was Constable Case Model.

I approached him. "Constable Case Model, how are you doing? What are you doing at the university?" I asked.

He looked confused. "Hi, who are you again?" Before I could answer, he continued. "I'm here as part of a community outreach program to talk to students about our activities."

I wondered if he remembered telling me I should aspire to do something useful like driving a cab. Instead, I said, "Tell me, Constable Case Model, are you still a racist?"

"No, no, you have it all wrong." He blushed and quickly washed his hands before walking out.

I stood there with my mouth agape. I wanted to continue the conversation. I wanted to ask him a million questions so that I could understand how he could do community outreach when he'd said so many awful things to us when we were at school. I was obvious that he had not remembered who I was, nor had he shown any awareness of what he had done to me and other friends with his white supremacist remarks when we were in high school. However, in the mirror I could see the look of anger rising in my face. It made me pause. I'd said what I'd most wanted to say to him. Something that had bugged me for years had been fixed. On second thought, nothing was fixed. But I had taken a step towards fixing it—I had named discrimination and challenged it without resorting to physical violence, as I might have done a few years ago.

Reporter and author Zuhair Kashmeri has written dozens of stories about violence, hatred, fear, and interrogation. In *The Gulf Within: Canadian Arabs, Racism and the Gulf War*, he looks at the work of a Montréal-based Arab Muslim psychiatrist who was working long hours to try to help people, including kids, who were suffering from the stress of being profiled and discriminated against. His examination of the Arab Muslim psyche, even among second- and third-generation Canadians, found that Arab Muslims in Canada were battered and brutalized, physically and emotionally. After the Gulf War, a national monitoring group, Muslim Media Watch, was established to address the negative portrayals of Islam being in the media.

What many people in our targeted community found just as frightening as the actual violence, was the silence. We were either too visible, and a target, or we were invisible, becoming mere shadows, or nothing, when we resisted victimization or needed healing. I know that there must've been organizations like CAFA or Al-Rashid Mosque that spoke for us, but it did not feel like we had much support. I will never forget how lonely and helpless I felt when all the people in charge, the ones I had learned to look up to, couldn't help. And that included police officers like Constable Case Model. Yes, his racist comments had spurred me on to complete ten years of university, to make something of myself, but humiliation is not a nourishing motivator.

In the lush North Saskatchewan River valley, at the Edmonton Heritage Festival in William Hawrelak Park, you can enjoy and get to know dozens of cultures—from the Ukrainian side of my friend Youssef's family to the Arab culture he and I share, and everything in between. There are many pavilions, performances, crafts, clothes, and food.

In 1996, while volunteering with Uncle Yazan at the Arabic pavilion, I began talking to a passerby. He was an older fellow, maybe in his seventies, and presented white.

"My great-grandfather was Lebanese," he told me.

"Oh, so you speak Arabic?" I asked.

"No," he replied. My family has lost touch with our Arab roots. I do remember my grandmother making us kibbeh and labneh when I was young. I would really like to know more about your culture."

I thought to myself, *This is my mother's worst nightmare for her children—needing to go a stranger to ask about our culture. How humiliating!* This man was several generations away from his Arab roots and all he had left was the memory of a few dishes. It was then that I began to understand why my parents had tried to instill these things in me—why they had done some of the things they did. That man in Hawrelak Park was seeking to fill a void, and I vowed that I would not let that happen to me or to my children. In response, I began to explore my cultural roots with renewed interest and began to notice how other Arab Canadians around me were losing their heritage.

In 1997, when I was in my second year of university, Edmonton hosted a national Canadian conference for Arab youth that had been organized by the Canadian Arab Federation. On the first night of the conference, a group of us went out to a restaurant. When the server came to take our drinks order after we sat down, I heard a young Lebanese woman say, "Yes, I'll have a beer, please." I stared at her, thinking my eyes and ears were playing tricks on me. I could not recall ever seeing an Arab woman drink alcohol, and most certainly not in public. I was shocked. I had grown up around the mosque, sheltered and supported by protective parents and tradition. For me and my friends, alcohol was completely off limits, and yet here this woman was, ordering a beer as if it was a glass of water. I knew not all Arabs were Muslims, and she may well have been a Christian, but I felt ashamed and embarrassed on her behalf. Slowly, I began to realize that the Arab community in Edmonton was in many ways more conservative and traditional than Arab communities elsewhere in Canada.

My undergraduate years changed me. I had been surprised that I had even been accepted into university and took the chance with my whole being. I really struggled during my first year. I had never really studied much at school and in my first year I struggled to come to terms with the change in culture from my school days. When I started, I still wanted to cause a bit of trouble and get up to mischief, but the other students were less accepting of bad behaviour than my school friends had been. I felt immature compared to them and began to take a close look at my behaviour and my actions. Over the course of that year, I slowly realized that the students around me, those who came from other communities, wanted to talk about science, politics, and religion, and not about who got shot or jumped. That was vastly different from my experience growing up in northeast Edmonton. where these were common topics of conversation. I began to surround myself with Arab youth who never got into trouble, and several of those people remain role models for me.

In my second year, I took my studies more seriously, and it paid off. Other students began to come to me for help. I liked being noticed for the good things I was doing, not for my rebellious past.

I graduated from the University of Alberta with a degree in Commerce, with distinction, specializing in management information systems. One day, a professor, Dr. Mike Carter, came to deliver a talk at the university about a master's program in health care information systems in the Department of Mechanical and Industrial Engineering at the University of Toronto. I applied and, to my surprise, got accepted into the program. Both my parents were proud of my achievement, and my mother wished me success in a new city, but my father struggled with the fact that it meant I would be leaving Edmonton. Our family was already broken up by the divorce, and he could not understand why I would want to move away and splinter it even further. But in the end, he realized I had to do what was best for my future.

On 25 August 1999, I packed my things and boarded a plane to Toronto. Except for our stopover on the way to Montréal when I was fifteen, I had never been in Toronto. Though I had moved out of home at age seventeen, this was the first time I had left Alberta on my own to live in another place. It felt like everything was being pulled away from under my feet, everything warm and familiar, even the things that bugged me.

I did not have much money, but I did have some papers that were priceless to me, especially a handwritten note in Arabic from my mother that I had received almost a year after she had moved to Vancouver with my brothers and sister.

Salam Alaikum wa Rahman Allahu wa Barakatu
[In the Name of Allah the Most Gracious and Most Merciful]

My Beloved Son, Mowafa,

I am writing this letter because I wanted to let you know that we are doing well in Vancouver. We have moved to the Vancouver suburb of Richmond, and we found a two-bedroom apartment where things are a little cramped, but for now it will suffice until things get better.

Your brother Belal is working part time at Bella Pizza. Omar is still engaging in his mischievous door-to-door chocolate almond sales. Saleh is going to school and Wafa is also doing well in high school and planning to go to Jordan this summer to visit family.

I know reading this letter is hard for you, as you may blame me for the separation of the family. I know that you are angry and upset with me. I just wanted to let you know that I never meant for this to happen. I always wanted our family to be together. I wanted to let you know that I love you and I am so sorry that you have to suffer alone as a result of what has happened.

Please do not worry about us, as Allah will take care of us. We live close to the mosque, and we try to go there as much as we can. I am teaching Arabic at the mosque and trying to register your brothers and sister into the Islamic program.

We are doing fine, and I want you to focus on your studies. I am so proud of you and what you are accomplishing in university. I know it has not been easy living alone, separated from us, but do not worry, we will be together soon. Just focus on your studies and your future for now.

My beloved son, I leave you now and I pray for your success. Remember to keep Allah present in your daily life and do not forget to do your daily prayers that will keep you connected with Allah.

I love you and pray for you . . .

Mom

《 · 》

I arrived in Toronto in late August with no place to live. A cab driver recommended a hostel. I sat there in a little single room, stunned and unprepared, my future hazy. I cried myself to sleep that first night. I felt alone and abandoned. I had lived alone for a year in Edmonton, but even then, friends and family were close. At university, I had shared accommodation with friends I could talk to. But now, for the first time in my life, I was truly on my own. There was one there to support me or ask me how I was doing. I felt helpless. All the emotions from the past two years— my parents' separation and my father's struggles—came crashing down on me.

On my second day in the city, I went to the University of Toronto; I discovered that there were students from over a hundred countries. I found the campus big and spread out, with a great contrast between old castle-like buildings covered in ivy that usually indicated arts and social science programs, and new buildings that generally indicated science and technology.

Waves of homesickness washed over me, and I felt dizzy and nauseated. Apart from those three years in Amman as a child and a few months in Montréal as a teenager, I hadn't lived anywhere other than Edmonton. I identified strongly with Edmonton's Castle Downs area—the malls, schools, and the Al-Rashid Mosque. Everything here was strange and unfamiliar. So I went to student housing. "We're so sorry, but you've arrived a little late. I don't know if there's anything we can help you with."

I grabbed a newspaper and found a place to sit on the green space near the huge Robarts Library. I felt dispirited as I started browsing the paper, looking for places to stay. I wanted to be close to the university so that I could engage easily and actively in the student community. I wanted somewhere I could fit in, and preferably a place where I could be among people who shared my faith and my cultural background, but I couldn't find anything like that.

I was still staying at the hostel, and I knew I needed to find more permanent accommodation before classes started in a few days' time. Sitting there on the lawn, I could see a large glass door about a hundred metres from the library. They led to a place called Ernescliff College. I did not know the place, but I thought it was worth going to see whether they had any places available. It was locked, but I pressed the doorbell. A gentleman in his forties opened the door and greeted me. I immediately felt better, though my heart was hammering inside my chest.

He introduced himself as the director of the college. His name was José. *Sounds like Househ,* I thought. José was from Peru. "Do you have any rooms for rent?" I said, my heart still pounding.

He smiled. "Yes, but we are very selective. We only take students with good marks and strong resumes. We want high achievers."

I told him that I had graduated with distinction from my university and that I had been accepted as a graduate student in engineering. That got me a tour of the place, a beautiful building with clean rooms, a gym, a small library, a meeting room, and even a prayer chapel. I asked him about the chapel. José said: "This is a Christian college, that is part of a Catholic organization, and we have rules for everyone who lives here."

I asked him what the rules were, wondering if I'd have to do something Christian. I could imagine my mother having fits.

"Good behaviour," he answered, "with a nightly curfew of 11 p.m. on weekdays and 1 a.m. on weekends, and participation in the nightly get-togethers. We are like a family, a home away from home."

Residency here included three meals a day, laundry, having your room cleaned three times a week, and even late-night snacks. At $750 a month, it sounded like a deal.

José gave me a form. "Complete this and send me your transcripts and your resume, and we will consider your application."

I filled out the application form and delivered it and a copy of my transcripts that same day. I was accepted. It was not the Muslim community I had set out to find, but at the time, finding a space in Ernescliff College felt more like an intervention from a higher being than a coincidence. After my night of loneliness, I had found a place that I could call home. In response to my father's struggles, and my own, I had increasingly explored piety in my own life, and at Ernescliff piety was a cornerstone of daily life. That appealed to me. So did the structured life—something I had not had before.

At Ernescliff, I lived with about fifty students and fifteen adults who worked for the church, as well as a handful of clergy who led worship in the faith of the Christian God. The religious adult staff all held prestigious positions in areas like engineering, music, public relations, and CEO headhunting, while the students were studying engineering, pre-med, English, and history.

The residence was associated with the Opus Dei organization, a controversial part of the Catholic Church. Opus Dei or
not, the Ernescliff College residence was, apart from the curfews, one of the best places I had ever lived in. I had thought it
would be difficult to adjust to living in such a deeply Christian
environment because even though Islam and Christianity are
both Abrahamic faiths, and the Islamic faithful share a belief
in the same monotheistic God as Christianity and Judaism, the
tenets of my faith differ significantly from these religions. Unlike
Christians, Muslims do not see Jesus (Issa in Arabic) as the son of
God who was sacrificed for humanity, but as a prophet. We regard
Muhammad as God's final messenger, and his teachings perme-
ate our whole culture and lifestyle—it is everything. Although our
faiths share the same roots in the Middle East, the history of our
relationship is complicated.

When I arrived at Ernescliff, I was told that we were expected
to practice our faith, and the faculty lived by example. Members
of Opus Dei follow the Catholic Liturgy of the Hours, which
requires the faithful to pray five times a day, much like Islam
requires the faithful to observe daily prayers. Even though life
at Ernescliff revolved around an expression of Catholic faith, no
one ever, directly or indirectly, tried to preach Christianity to me.
However, the resident priest, Father Craig, did ask me regularly if
I was doing my Muslims prayers, which I confess I was not really
doing at the time, with the exception of the Friday prayer.

At Ernescliff we were all here for a specific purpose—to go
to school, to work and live together. Every night, we would sit
down together as a group, and everyone would talk about what
they had done that the day. It was like being part of a family. We
were expected to dress for mealtimes, especially Sunday din-
ners. I remember coming to dinner one Sunday wearing sweats
and a T-shirt and being asked to go change into something more

appropriate. My mother had brought me up to show respect and self-respect, but Ernescliff worked on a different level, and it was a shock to adapt to this more formal environment.

Despite what I'd achieved in university to that point in my life, spending so much time among high-achieving students often made me feel like a country hick from Western Canada who had come to the big city not knowing much. While I was happy on many levels at Ernescliff, I struggled to fit in intellectually. Being among all those high-achieving peers made me feel that somehow I had been disadvantaged growing up in an immigrant family in the north side of Edmonton. The other residents at Ernescliff seemed so intelligent and intellectual, and used words I did not understand and had never heard before. I remember we were watching a hockey game one day. When my team, the Edmonton Oilers, scored I would yell things like "Awesome!" or "Amazing!" When the other team scored, their supporters used words I'd never heard before, like "stupendous" and "astonishing" to describe a goal.

I tried to become more intellectual by hanging around them and listening to their conversations, but I longed to learn more about my own culture, too, so I started looking for opportunities to engage more with Arabic culture. Among the confusion of groups at the U of T International Centre, including the Ahmadiyya Muslim Students' Association and the Twelve Imams Muslim Students' Association, it was the Muslim Students' Association (MSA) that sounded the most similar to the group I had been involved in in Edmonton, so I joined.

I encountered many other kinds of groups, too. Secular groups that I had not been aware of, like the Rotary Club. One day, I started talking to a man who was a member of the Rotary Club. He told me they had a grant for students with high marks who were in financial need and encouraged me to apply. Three weeks later, I received a cheque for three thousand dollars. I still wish I could thank him in person. With that money, I was able to pay for a few more months at the Ernescliff College residence and finally felt that I would get by in Toronto.

As I moved deeper into university life, I began to meet more people I could identify with, one of whom was Abdul Razzak Takriti. A second-year undergraduate student in political science and history, he frequently wore the Palestinian keffiyeh, especially during the cold winter months. It was easy to find him in a crowd. He came from a wealthy Jordanian family and was an ambitious young man who was out to change the world. After finishing his master's degree, he went on to the Oxford University for his PhD.

One night in Toronto, I met with him and another fellow, Muhammad, at one of the university's restaurant pubs for an Arab Student Association party. I wasn't used to these kinds of parties. For one thing, they served alcohol, and I found myself staring at men and women partying, drinking, dancing, and talking to each other very freely. Back home in Edmonton, even though the University of Alberta Arab Student Association and the Canadian Arab Friendship Association were seen by the some as liberal, our events never had alcohol. There had always been parents at the larger functions, and girls were chaperoned by their brothers, who took their duty seriously. We might call Islam a religion of peace, but there would be no peace for the guys who went after our sisters. Being at this MSA event in Toronto felt more like being at a nightclub. While I was playing pool, I asked a guy, "Isn't this kind of strange and different from our culture?"

He aimed the cue, slammed a ball into the pocket, and then grinned and said, "I have no problem with this. It's normal." Others agreed and even seemed surprised that I asked. I began to feel like even more of a conservative, constrained Arab red-neck from Alberta. I could feel my skin prickle. I asked one guy whose sister was at the party, "Aren't you worried if someone flirts with her?" He shrugged and said, "Hey, it's her life and I'm okay with it."

One day, I was sitting in a Toronto café with my friend Abdul and a few other people. They were getting loud about American intervention in the Middle East and how the United States was a colonial superpower that has caused much more harm than good in the world. I told them what my father had told me about receiving USAID donations in the refugee camp in Amman, Jordan. They all laughed. "Yes, that is fine, and it helped your father and others survive day-to-day but look at the larger picture. America has damaged the world by acting as an intervening power in the world, dictating how every region should be run."

While feeling like an idiot, I could see the truth in this.

The discussion piqued my curiosity. I wanted to learn more. Abdul suggested that I read a book called *Orientalism*, by Edward Said, a Palestinian-American scholar and public intellectual. The book describes the subtle but strong Eurocentric prejudice shown towards Arab Islamic people and their cultures, which are often seen as exotic and backwards. Said demonstrates how colonial powers control knowledge production in universities and in media representations. Abdul also recommended other books with similar themes—like Noam Chomsky's *Manufacturing Consent: The Political Economy of the Mass Media*, which looks at the propaganda, distortion, and corporate sponsorship of major news outlets.

As I was reading these books, I realized how limited my vocabulary was. I was intellectually small, a puny cardamom seed. I bought an Oxford dictionary and proceeded to write down any word I didn't understand in a notebook. Within a few months, I had collected over two thousand words. I began to read voraciously, going to the dictionary over and over, trying to understand and use more words. Still, my health policy professors, who I looked up to since they advocated for quality in public health care, told me that my writing was under par for a graduate student.

So I bought *A Canadian Writer's Reference* and soaked up grammar, basic sentence structure, vocabulary, and referencing styles. I became more confident and wrote articles for newspapers, as well as letters to the editor. It became clear to me how important writing skills are to success in university programs, and though my surname means "confused," I was determined that my writing wouldn't reflect that. I was also coming back to the energy I had for writing when I was a kid, before other people's assumptions got in the way.

I had already come a long way since Edmonton. Reading books and meeting with people who knew more than I did constantly reminded me that I could have been born a struggling Palestinian in a camp, and this encouraged me to work harder.

In Toronto, my hunger for learning more about Islam, Arab culture, and the history of my people continued to grow. I began to attend various lectures outside of the university classes I was taking. Uncle Yazan had told me about some of the people I head about in these talks, like the great twelfth-century Muslim leader Saladin. I began to look for more. On eBay, along with some old Arabic coins, I found two books that I came to treasure—one by Abu l-Walid Muhammad bin Ahmad bin Rushd, also known as Ibn Rushd or Averroes, and one by the great Muslim philosopher, Ibn Khaldun.

Reading these books about two exceptional Muslims who helped shape European thinking, I could not help but think, *Why wasn't I ever taught about them in school?* Averroes was a great twelfth-century Muslim scholar who wrote more than sixty-seven original works—twenty thousand pages covering a variety of subjects, including early Islamic philosophy, logic in Islamic philosophy, Arabic medicine, mathematics, astronomy, grammar, Islamic theology, Sharia (Islamic law), Fiqh (Islamic jurisprudence), and grammar, as well as commentaries on most of Aristotle's works and on Plato's *Republic*.

I found myself shutting out the world and disappearing into this new world of knowledge I had discovered. Over a thousand years ago, I learned, the city of Baghdad contained Bayt al-Hikma (The House of Wisdom), which was considered the top intellectual establishment of the time. It held one of the greatest collections of knowledge in the world, with books on every subject and in many languages. There were so many scholars that this library had to keep building and expanding to contain all that world knowledge. I kept going back to things like the pharmacy section, thinking, *Yaba, what an ancient and honourable profession you chose.*

There was so much I had never been exposed to in high school and university. It was if Muslims, Islam, and the Arabs had been wiped out of the whole curriculum. I was taught about the Jewish Holocaust but not the tragedy of the Nakba; about the persecution of Jews during the Spanish Inquisition, but not about the persecution of Muslims and the push to expel them from the Spanish mainland. And so it continued from my backyard in Edmonton to the West Bank: I could see attempt after attempt to destroy Arabic peoples and cultures, but nothing that would acknowledge the many contributions Muslims had made to Western culture.

What I was hearing now, as an Arab Muslim in Canada, was "You are a threat to us" or "You are at the bottom of the ladder, below the first rung, in the dirt," like in the Israeli-occupied territories of Palestine. So many questions arose within me and the need to find answers grew stronger.

During the summer of 2000, I left Ernescliff and found a place to stay in a mixed dormitory in Trinity College. After living in a men's only environment, I found it difficult to adjust. I was shocked, for instance, to see women walking around in their underwear, and even more so by the fact that it did not seem to bother a friend of mine who came from Jordan. One night, I locked myself out of my dormitory and had to sleep on the couch. It was clear other students had had a party and had not cleaned up, for there were beer bottles everywhere. In the morning, one of the nuns walked in and saw me lying there in the midst of all these bottles. She accused me of irresponsible behaviour even though she knew I did not drink. Then she left and came back with signs that said DRINK IN MODERATION, which she put up all over the place. It hurt to see how easily she had made assumptions and put the blame on me.

One night towards the end of my graduate studies, I watched the movie *Malcolm X* with some of the other people in my dormitory. It affected me deeply, and the very next day I went out to buy Alex Haley's *The Autobiography of Malcolm X*. I read passages from the book over and over. Halfway through the book, I started to really understand what Malcolm X meant about the struggle against white people. There were not many whom he found good in his life; instead, they used Black people as they saw fit—exploiting and destroying them.

In school, Malcolm X was told he might become a carpenter if he was lucky—certainly not a lawyer, which he longed to be. This brought to mind Uncle Faisal, who had to leave school to help support his family in the Palestine refugee camp and become a carpenter. Whether it was history, philosophy, African languages, law, the Muslim faith, or any other subject you could imagine, Malcolm X was determined to study it, to raise himself above what white people told him he could be. To me, one of the best statements in his autobiography is this: "I would just like to *study*. I mean ranging study, because I have a wide-open mind. I'm interested in almost any subject you can mention."

That was what I felt in Toronto. I cry inside for those who have education denied to them. Education and being able to read is a weapon and a path towards healing. I can only imagine how students at the schools in Gaza and other terrorized zones feel when their buildings and classrooms are bombed and annihilated, ending up a heap of brick and glass, littered with charred scraps of paper. Like a flaming blockade of tires rolled into the streets, I was spinning, with questions burning inside me.

I had finally found positive motivation from the late Edward Said. Three of his many books—*Orientalism*; *Covering Islam: How the Media and the Experts Determine How We See the Rest of the World*; and his autobiography, *Out of Place*—were especially influential for me. In addition to the brilliance of his writing and debating, I appreciated him for his ability to live in two worlds, English and Arabic, all the while being an advocate for the Palestinian cause.

Before he passed away, I had the opportunity to see Said speak in Toronto and was inspired by how he connected his struggles with identity and language to his practice as an academic. He told the audience that universities are part of the system of elite knowledge production that constructs a Western understanding of the East to further the goals of imperialism. He encouraged us to work from both inside and outside universities to decode the discrimination that has become accepted as curriculum. As I listened to him speak, and let his writing sink into my life, I became aware of how I had been mocked for the way I spoke English, for my faith and for my culture. I realized how these things made me an outsider in Canada despite my status as a citizen, and how those at the centre of power used my position as an immigrant as a sword against me. I began to realize that language could be used as a gate to keep certain groups excluded or stereotyped as "uncivilized" foreigners or as immigrants who have not contributed to humanity's collective knowledge, or to their adopted homes.

Through Said and Malcom X, I began to see myself differently and to have a faith in my abilities that I did not have before. I felt both comforted and upset by Said's insights, which helped me to understand the injustice that lay at the root of my family's past, present, and future experiences.

In 2013, Najla Said, Edward Said's daughter and a renowned academic, playwright, actor, and activist in her own right, published a memoir. Though her background, gender, and religion are different from mine, her book, *Looking for Palestine: Growing Up Confused in an Arab-American Family*, made me shake with understanding: *Yes! That's exactly how it is! I know what she means!* With such books, how can we forget a culture, or pretend it does not exist, in all its diverse transnational forms? Feeling such a deep connection with literature and the life stories of people like me helped me continue to pursue my own career as a researcher and teacher.

In December 1999, I returned to Edmonton for a visit. I joined Talal, the Lebanese Ukrainian who was my old roommate at the University of Alberta, and his cousin Youssef at a local twenty-four-hour diner on the northside of Edmonton. On that particular night, it was packed, and we were enjoying our burgers, minding our own business, when a man at a table across from ours suddenly stood up and said in a loud voice, "I'm a gonna go to Bosnia and kill you Muslims."

We stopped eating. The whole restaurant paused and looked at the spectacle that was unfolding. One of the other people at his table looked embarrassed. "Sorry about that," he said to us. "My soldier friend is drunk."

Youssef was upset. He wanted to say something, but Talal and I stopped him. Then I did exactly what I'd just cautioned Youssef not to do. I spoke up.

"You know what?" I said to the soldier, "I don't blame you for speaking like that because your father probably spoke in the same manner. Please sit down, thank you very much." Part of me wanted to add, "My friend here is part Ukrainian, as many of you are, too!" But it didn't feel like that would translate.

His friend pulled him back into his seat, but the man stood up again and repeated his words: "I'm gonna to go to Bosnia to kill you Muslims."

Again the restaurant went quiet. Still no one in the entire restaurant said a word. The man's friend, the one who had apologized earlier, apologized once more for his friend. Then the soldier yelled out for a third time. The tension at our table was palpable. What hurt most was the quiet complicity of all those who were watching the sequence of events. Youssef was ready to explode. "One more time, and I'm going to beat him up," he muttered.

I asked the server to call someone, the police perhaps, but she shot back that the man was drunk and not hurting anyone. A few minutes later, the man made another obscene outburst about Muslims. This time Youssef jumped up.

"If you want to start killing Muslims, why don't you start with me? Let's go outside."

Almost everyone in the restaurant spoke up.

"Let him be."

"Leave him alone, he's drunk."

These people had all been silent when he was threatening to kill Muslims. You could say it was because of the innate Canadian sense of politeness, but they were quite ready to speak up in his defence when the target of man's racial abuse stood up to respond. Just like that, Youssef had become the bad guy.

Youssef and the other man stormed outside to fight, but Talal and I stayed behind. Out of the corner of my eye, I saw the waitress speaking on the phone. She had called the police. I knew how this would end. I'd seen it happen many times before. I knew if the police came and saw a "Leb" apparently bashing a white man, they would put him in jail. And us, too, if we were anywhere near them. Talal and I stood up and went outside. Youssef and the other guy were pushing each other around. We dragged Youssef away before the police came.

We may not have ended up in prison that night, but it certainly felt like we might as well have escaped from one if the derisive looks people gave us on the way out of the restaurant was anything to go by.

NORTH

الشمال

11

Flying to Amman

As I was finishing my degree at the University of Toronto, I began reading more about Palestine and my desire to return to my ancestral home got stronger. It was a call to me, like the *adhan*. I wanted to go to Palestine and get to know more about my people first-hand. I wanted to know more about my cultural heritage and the suffering of my people. I had saved up a little money, and I finally made a conscious decision. "I'm going to return to Palestine," I told my friends and family. "I can take care of myself, and I can be a bridge between people, using my fluency in Arabic and English. I will document it somehow."

"But you are not a journalist."

"No, but there are ways to do this online . . ."

Towards the middle of September 2000, I boarded a plane heading to France for the first leg of my journey. I was aware of the many Arab and Muslim brothers and sisters with me on the flight, but I didn't feel like talking to them. I wanted to be in my own little world, but the close quarters on an airplane don't always allow it. The Texan sitting beside me was planning to tour Eastern Europe, Russia, and the Middle East, and I heard about it at length.

He didn't ask me about my travel plans, but I'd given myself a project called "Compare life as a Palestinian Canadian in Canada to life as a Canadian Palestinian in Palestine." Uncle Yazan had challenged me to write about the suffering of Palestinians in the occupied territories. In some ways, I was going to a place where I belonged, yet my impressions, beyond being in Jordan for three years as a child, had been formed mainly by the Western media. I had begun to understand the art of media spin. The camera shot that says a thousand words, often none of them good. The mind that arrives at a conflict scene already made up. The pro-Israeli bias in the media that showed Israelis looking "civilized" and Palestinians looking angry, yelling, with scarves tied around their heads and faces, to give the impression that most Palestinians would bomb people in public places and kill themselves doing it. I wanted to go where I could dig behind those biased reports.

My parents and friends weren't entirely on board with my plans.

"You want to go to the Middle East *now*?"

"Look at what you're getting into. What if you find yourself in the middle of a war?"

"Mowafa, you are going at such a sensitive time, when so many things could happen. I don't think it's wise. If you must go, go for a quick visit and come home."

"It will always be sensitive there," I replied. "I may never have this chance again."

For months, Palestinian people had been preparing for large-scale protests against the Israeli Defense Forces if the peace talks floundered. The Israelis had certainly been doing the same and had been chasing the pump, as bodybuilders say, by stocking up on billions of dollars' worth of military equipment given to them by the United States. My dad said he would rather I stayed home and worked.

He was afraid for me, and he was thinking like most fathers would—if your kids have the opportunity, they should work, make money, get married, have kids, carve out a future. But he also knew I had to do this. It wasn't just that I was the firstborn, the oldest son, and had his name as my middle name. I was also at the age and time of life when this trip was most possible. I had finished my degree and was thinking about grad school and settling down in a few years' time. The time for Palestine was now.

My plan was to go to Al-Quds, the capital of Palestine (known in the West as Jerusalem) and find an inexpensive hostel there. My ultimate goal was to offer the *isha*, the daily nighttime prayer, at Al-Masjid al-Aqsa, which was located on the Haram esh-Sharif, the Temple Mount.

As the plane crossed the Atlantic Ocean towards the Middle East, I could feel myself reaching into the past, becoming an extension of my ancestors. As I was wrapping up my graduate studies in Toronto, I felt a strong urge to study Arabic and religion, and for me that also meant connecting with my cultural and political heritage. There was no better place to do that than in Palestine, I'd reasoned, and so here I was on my way to take courses in Islamic studies and Arabic at the Islamic University of Gaza. Though I'd lived in Jordan as a child for three years, had heard Arabic at home constantly, and could speak it at the mosque, it was not enough for me. I also wanted to learn more about Islam at Al-Aqsa, and the time felt right. The Camp David Summit had taken place in July 2000, with US president Bill Clinton, Israeli prime minister Ehud Barak, and Palestinian Authority president Yasser Arafat meeting in hopes of negotiating a peace settlement. During those meetings, four major items became four big obstacles: territory/borders, Jerusalem and the Haram esh-Sharif, refugees and the "right of return," and Israeli security concerns.

The photos of the three leaders standing around in casual clothes in the woodland like old friends did not tell the whole story. In the end, the Camp David Summit of 2000 was a failure, just as the Oslo Conference of 1993 and the Camp David Summit of 1978 had been, and other summits before, between, and after. The problem was always the same: the most that the Israelis were willing to give did not meet the least that the Palestinians were asking for. Two things the Palestinians wanted were a reversion to the lines of 1967 (the year of the Israeli-Arab Six-Day War) and recognition of the "right of return" for Palestinian refugees. Bill Clinton tried floating a "bridging proposal," which would result in additional flexibility on territory, and some EU observers reported that Israel would accept the idea of East Jerusalem as the capital of a Palestinian state.

I held to a youthful optimism that voices of passion and reason would prevail and that matters would be resolved. I needed to assess the situation with my own eyes. It was easy to be critical in a classroom on the other side of the world, but in the end being on the street in Palestine would give me the best understanding of the situation.

If the peace talks failed, I knew I would likely be travelling into a large-scale conflict. People living in impoverished camps would never see the Palestine that was taken from them. The new regime would suppress them further, and the Palestinian economy would continue to decline, and Palestinians would not take that suppression lying down.

At the time I arrived in Jerusalem, the *Waqf,* the Islamic religious endowment, was conducting extensive construction on the Masjid al-Aqsa. Muslims call it the Noble Sanctuary—Bait-ul-Muqaddas. It marks the location of Muḥammad's arrival in Jerusalem and his ascent to heaven, and is the third holiest site in Islam, after Mecca and Medina. The same site is considered so holy by Jews (who call it *Har HaBáyit*, the Mount of the House of God), that they will not walk there. Because of its significance for both Judaism and Islam, sovereignty over the Haram esh-Sharif is a major point of contention. Both Israel and the Palestinian Authority claim sovereignty over it, and it lies at the centre of the ongoing Arab-Israeli conflict, both geographically and emotionally.

One of the people I connected with before I left Toronto was journalist and consultant Mark Bruzonsky. The tagline for his website is "News, Views, and Analysis Governments, Lobbies, and Associated Interest Groups Don't Want You to Know." Mark's perspectives amazed me and reminded me to get to know Jews as well as Arabs in the Middle East. The challenge might be finding ordinary Jews to talk to, as opposed to people who were part of the powerful Israeli elite.

With degrees in international affairs and law from Princeton and New York University, Mark has written and spoken for many years about world affairs, US foreign policy, the Middle East, the underlying realities of policymaking in Washington, and US-Israeli relations. When I contacted him in 2000, he was also producer and host of the weekly TV program *Mid-East Realities*. He has travelled to over forty-five countries and has been the official guest of many organizations (such as the PLO) and governments, including those of Egypt, Libya, Sudan, and Saudi Arabia.

Until the Jewish Committee on the Middle East had to end its activities in 1994, Mark was chair of this group, the first American Jewish organization to call for a fully sovereign and independent Palestinian state. JCOME's statement of principles was published in more than fifty mainstream newspapers and magazines, including the *New York Review of Books*. It's difficult for an Arab cause to get fair mainstream coverage, so this was a big deal.

It's the kind of thing that gives you great hope for even the possibility of understanding and resolution, I wrote in my journal at the time.

I had always thought that all or most Jews hated Arabs and Muslims—because Israel had stolen our land and displaced our people. It's true that my father had a Jewish friend or two, and my Uncle Faisal had worked with an Edmonton rabbi as part of the outreach work in their respective communities of faith until the Israeli war in Lebanon caused a disagreement between them. If Mark Bruzonsky had been an Arab or Muslim criticizing his own people, he would have been ostracized from the community, as I suspected he had been from his own Jewish community. But here was a person who wanted to help and make a difference, despite that cost.

Mark suggested I read David Fromkin's *A Peace to End All Peace: The Fall of the Ottoman Empire and the Creation of the Modern Middle East.* Fromkin's book, a finalist for the Pulitzer Prize, looks at how the dissolution of the Ottoman Empire during World War I led to great changes in the Middle East as it was carved out by the Allies. He explores the role played by European powers in creating the Middle East as it is today, with the Sykes-Picot Agreement and the signing of the Balfour Declaration, which promised land for Jewish people in historic Palestine. That signalled the beginning of ongoing Arab-Israeli conflicts and hostilities and remains a major source of dissent. This context and this history should have been clear indicators of what would happen after the current "peace process" had run its course. I was heading into a volatile environment without a full understanding of the history. I would catch up quickly.

I could feel my body tense up as I listened to Ben, the American seated next to me on the second leg of my flight to Israel, talk about the Middle East. "All empires seek influence," he said, "so American intervention in world politics is only normal. Think objectively." As if that made it all right that Palestine's borders were redrawn after World War II, that Israel was granted Palestinian land, and that the Palestinians became refugees in the aftermath of what had happened to European Jews.

Something was really wrong. So many of the current European settler Jews had little connection with citizens of Israel—and there were a few Jewish people who were not Zionists, who did not approve of the creation of a state at the expense of Indigenous people. But people like Ben think we should be "objective." *It's the kind of thing that could drive a Muslim to drink,* I thought as the flight attendant rolled the cart by my seat.

When I had fought back in school, people who saw me might have thought, "How typical. They start young. Troublemakers. Aggressive and uncivilized!" Yet being quiet and invisible doesn't work either. "What is he planning? What is he plotting? Skulking around like that. Why doesn't he talk to us and reassure us, if he's not a terrorist in training?" Whether out in the open as an Arab or trying not to be openly Arab, we could never do the right thing. There is no place to go.

I was going to leave all that behind for a few months and see what kind of person I was in Palestine. I tried not to think of my mother worrying about me and talking endlessly to all her friends about it, and even to my dad, though they were divorced. There was enough worry when I was growing up, before university. I hoped instead that, whatever other feelings they had, they would feel proud of me for "going home." I thought especially of my dad, whose birthplace was a mere twelve kilometres from where this airplane would land.

12

Welcome to Al-Quds

Ben-Gurion Airport is located near the "suburb" of Lod, Israel, once known as Lydda, Palestine. This is the village of my father's and grandfather's family, who were expelled that summer of 1948. My father has never been able to return. Lydda was the last town to fall during the Nakba. Perhaps not surprisingly, among all the "Welcome to Israel" signs in the airport, there is nothing to indicate that 700,000 Palestinians were driven away, and that death, displacement, or refugee status has followed them ever since their eviction from an ancestral home.

I could still remember how sick I'd felt arriving in Toronto as an Albertan Arab hick. It was the first time I had taken a long flight on my own away from Edmonton. Here, at the Israeli-managed customs control, I was nervous in a different way. It was as if I had "Up with Palestine!" stamped across my chest. Standing in line, I noticed that some people moved quickly through customs. Jews were asked a few questions and left to proceed; everything was calm, efficient, and dignified.

An African American and I were not so lucky. We were both interrogated by security agents as if they were being paid by the question. "Where are you going? What is the purpose of your visit? Where does your family live? Where does your family come from?" The minutes dragged on.

The officer continued to ask probing questions, and I kept telling her that I was going to be studying at the Islamic University of Gaza. Eventually, the ordeal stopped. As I gathered my belongings, I asked the security agent why she had questioned me so thoroughly. "You weren't special," she said, as if that explained everything. And in a way, it did. In 1995, Fatah, a Palestinian political party that was aligned with Yasser Arafat's PLO, had supported the Interim Agreement on the West Bank and the Gaza Strip, commonly known as Oslo II, which not only legitimized a Jewish state on the 78 percent of Palestinian land Israel had occupied since 1947, but had offered them an additional 12 percent, which left Palestinians with less than 10 percent of their original country. After the failure at Camp David, many Fatah factions had deserted the party and joined Hamas, which did not support the Oslo II Accord. In this destabilized environment between the Camp David Summit and my arrival at Ben-Gurion Airport, one or more of these factions had launched attacks on Israel. The additional scrutiny was part of Israel's heightened vigilance in the wake of these attacks.

I finally got through customs and took a shuttle bus to downtown Jerusalem. After the thirteen-hour flight, I needed a meal. "I want to go to Old Jerusalem," I said to the driver. "Ya, ya, ya!" he said over the cranked-up Klezmer tunes. He insisted on fifteen US dollars for the ride, when I had been told it should be only ten. I was not willing to pay the extra fee, so I turned away. One man on the bus said, "You know what you should have done to him—punch him." All I could do was force a smile and wave my hand dismissively, as though it wasn't worth my time.

I got on another bus and asked the driver if it was going to Jerusalem Square. I remembered those questions at the airport:

"Why are you visiting? Why are you here? Where will you be staying?" I hadn't planned the specific details in advance. I had only decided to go a week before I booked my trip, so I was lucky to have come this far after the security grilling. I knew only that I wanted to go straight to the Old City. When I got off the bus, I found a hostel close to the city gates, checked in, and went out to find some food.

My hostel was located almost in the shadow of the Haram esh-Sharif, right by the Masjid al-Aqsa. As I sat in a nearby café, a man came out of nowhere and began telling me story after story of people he had helped. My eyes were glazed with jetlag. I was not taking in much of what he was saying, but it did not take him long to discover that I came from Canada. That was when he began asking things like, "Can you help me go to Canada? How can I do it?"

"I can't get you there," I said, "but take this." I gave him the contact information for the Canadian Arab Friendship Association and told him to talk to Yazan Haymour. I figured Uncle Yazan would know what to do.

Despite the masjid being just steps away, I missed the prayers at Masjid al-Aqsa on the first day of my time in Palestine. So I went to find some breakfast and figure out my next steps. I ordered coffee and stared at the shops and restaurants around me, the colours and motion blurring together. As I sat drinking my coffee, I heard two guys chatting away about Palestine in a mix of English and in Arabic. They saw me staring at them and smiled. "Won't you join us?"

I spent the rest of the day chatting and arguing with Wael and his friend Michael, a Palestinian Christian lawyer who had been educated in the United States. When Michael left, Wael and I carried on talking. As I got up to leave to return to my hostel, I told Wael that he had convinced me to register at Al-Quds University as soon as possible to study Arabic and religion.

"No," Wael replied, "you will stay at my place, and I'll help you to register."

Wael shared an apartment with a friend in Abu Dis, a suburb of Jerusalem. I began to refuse, saying it was too much trouble, but my resistance was half-hearted. I had heard about Abu Dis because it had been suggested as a potential location for the Palestinian capital. Wael was persistent, and it did not take long for me to agree to stay at his place for the night. I retrieved my suitcase from the hostel while he found a servees—a minibus taxi—to take us to Abu Dis. Fear came creeping back. He seemed like a good guy, but I began praying to myself, thinking of my mother and father. Would they be bringing my body back home, if I could even be identified, or if there was even a body to find? Would I end up one of those people who mysteriously disappears when far from home?

The ride to Abu Dis was a dark one, with the lights of Jerusalem fading away as we entered the Israeli-controlled Palestinian suburb. By the time the servees finally stopped at a four-storey apartment building, my mind was whirling, and my palms were slippery with sweat. Wael insisted on paying for the servees.

Wael and his roommate, Muhammad, showed me to my room. The barking and howling of wild dogs outside did nothing to settle my mind. I was exhausted but restless, thinking about how Israel had renegotiated a new deadline with the PLO, how the Palestinians were to be given their freedom by this day, 13 September 2000. What would the morning and the days ahead bring? I got up and prayed and asked God to take care of me. I also thought about how great it would be to be able to send home news about Palestinian freedom to my father. He—and others, like Uncle Faisal—said they hoped things would improve here as they said goodbye to me in Edmonton.

The next morning, Wael suggested I move in with them.

I thanked him for his kind offer but told him I wanted to stay in the Old City for a while so I could be close to the masjid and get to know the place before making final decisions about where to live.

According to Israeli myths, the country of Palestine was mostly an empty desert, inhabited by a few struggling Palestinian villages, until the Israelis came along and, with their agricultural methods, redeemed the arable land before it was too late. What they were doing, they said, was superior to what the native farmers like my grandfather had done. Even during the British Mandate, Israel tried to convince the world that Palestine was an uninhabited desert, "a land without people for a people without a land." This *terra nullius* concept has been used many times to defend colonization, including in Canada to justify the occupation of the Prairies and their transformation into the Canadian "breadbasket." As I discovered the many historical buildings and sites of Palestine, I kept confirming that this story was the real myth.

Wael often came to spend time with me in the Old City, and we became good friends. One day, Wael and I talked late into the evening once more. It would be a struggle for him to find transport back to his house at that time of night, so I suggested he stay at a hostel with me so that we could continue our conversation. We found a hostel in the northern part of Jerusalem's Old City and asked for rooms for the night. The manager looked at my Canadian passport and was happy to have me stay at the hostel, but he would not let Wael stay there. "No Arabs allowed," he kept saying. Mowafa and Wael. Both Palestinian names, belonging to people who both look Middle Eastern. It made no sense, except in Al-Quds: Wael had grown up in Jenin, whereas I was from Canada. With a shrug, this manager told me to try other hostels, so we did. But it was the same: they would accept me, but not my friend, my fellow traveller, my brother. One meaning of the Arabic name Wael is "seeking shelter," and yet that is the one thing that was eluding us.

Eventually, we did find a hostel. It was rundown and clearly needed the business. The person at reception reluctantly allowed both of us to stay for one night, but the reaction was still nasty. If this had happened in Canada, I would have given the person behind the counter a piece of my mind, but in in Al-Quds, things were different, I'd realized.

As I was getting into bed, I asked Wael, "How do you feel?"

"Oppressed. Hurt." I could feel the pain in his gestures, his voice, and his eyes. He then turned over and we both went to sleep, or at least he did. I was fuming. I wanted to destroy my passport, that piece of paper that made me look as though I was better than my brother. I thought to myself, *The worst thing he's probably done is drink alcohol, and only God knows the trouble and havoc I caused as a teenager growing up in Canada.* I swear, Wael's little toe was worth four of me. I got quite worked up, thinking of him here, oppressed, while I lived a very different life in Canada, complete with freedoms and at least a superficial sense of happiness despite the threats, stigma, and displacement that strained my family. Across from each other in the hostel bunk beds, I was a world away from this stranger who was treating me as a brother. That was when I decided to ask Wael if the offer to stay with them was still open.

13

The Children of Palestine

The unarmed Intifada produced poignant cultural artifacts, many of which are freely available on the Internet. As I browse the Internet, I can look at photographs of Palestinian children from the First Intifada. I see kids the same age as I was when I lived with my family in Amman, Jordan. Dressed in yellow shorts, T-shirt, and sandals, one youth is aiming a stone at a huge Israeli tank. If I had been a youth in Palestine at that time, I might have been one of the children following orders to roll tires onto roads, pour gasoline on them, and set them on fire. Even Ehud Barak, a former Israeli prime minister, once said, "If I were a Palestinian of the right age, I would join, at some point, one of the 'terrorist' groups."

The posters I think of most often as I reflect on my time in Palestine show kids with slingshots and burning tires, and a boy in profile, holding up his hand against Israeli soldiers and a tank. "An Unceasing Intifada Will Defeat the Occupation," says the writing underneath his picture. Another poster declares, "Palestinian Children Are Stronger Than the Occupation," and I have no doubt that is true. Like most Palestinians, both in Palestine and in the diaspora, I do not wish for the conflict to continue endlessly, but I also know that the resistance to occupation must be sustained.

I know in my heart that in every Palestinian generation there will be a group of children, men, women, and organizations that will lead that resistance.

While I was in Palestine during the days leading up to the Second Intifada and the days immediately following the protests that broke out shortly after my arrival, I met many Palestinian children who had grown up in an environment of permanent war and occupation, and even some who had been shot at by Israeli soldiers. Even as they lived in despair, or perhaps *because* they lived in despair, I was surprised by how they still managed to behave like children anywhere else in the world, getting into arguments with their siblings and their friends. Occasionally, I would try to talk with them and get them to make peace, but as I walked away, I would see them going at it again.

The resilience these children show under these circumstances made me wonder who the intended audience was for some of the posters about kids being "stronger than the occupation"— the Israelis and the uncaring world at large, or those of us who doubt the resilience of children. Was it to reassure parents their kids would survive? Or was it to encourage children whose parents were missing, imprisoned, or murdered? I do not know the answers to these questions, but I do know this: those children will survive. I remember giving some kids on the streets money and being surprised when they threw it back at me. Once, I paid a young vendor for a box of Kleenex, but conveniently forgot to take them when I left. He ran after me and shoved it in my hand.

"I'm a businessman," he said. "I don't need handouts."

I soon learned that handouts insulted their dignity and took away their pride. They would not take handouts, not from me, and not from the Israelis. These children will continue to fight until the last occupier leaves.

≪ · ≫

While I lived with Wael in Abu Dis, I made an effort every day to take a servees to the Old City to attend prayers at the holiest of masjids. Going to Al-Aqsa usually cleared my mind, at least for a while.

On my second morning with my new friends, I woke up not knowing where I was. I had dreamt of meeting Tuma, my grandfather. The dream was still with me as I turned on the tap full blast to wash my face. I wished he and all his loved ones could drink it, splash in it, make tea with it, and take a hot shower to wash all the dust and fatigue away.

My father and Uncle Faisal told me there had been times when there was too much water—when water dripped, even poured, through the leaky roof of the refugee camp tent. Sometimes people would catch some in containers. Being forced to move again, though, meant they were often thirsty; at the most desperate times, like when they were on the death march leaving Lydda, they had to drink urine. Sometimes they would find a well and suck the water off the clothes of the kid who had been lowered down to get the first scoop.

I dried my face, and then set out for the masjid.

After morning prayers, I walked through the Old City. Walking along Jaffa Street, I was surrounded by Western-type venues that were clearly geared to tourists. It struck me that I was one of those tourists, and I vowed I would get to experience the Palestine that lay beyond the tourist sites. It was still early, but it was already scorching, hotter than Edmonton in summer. Alberta had the Prairies, but this place had the desert. I felt parched and dehydrated. I walked into a pub and asked for a glass of water.

The occupation has affected Palestinian access to water significantly. My grandfather had been a farmer, living free, and in later life, a gardener. He always had access to water. Now, Israeli settlers get their water from more than forty "deep holes"—plenty for gardens, swimming pools, and miles of crops and greenhouses. If Tuma were alive today, he would not be able to access this life source. The Israeli military routinely destroys Palestinian water tanks as part of their rules of occupation. Palestinians have to get permits to dig wells, and the red tape involved in getting such a permit makes it almost impossible.

I was thirsty every day. Back home, clean water just comes gushing out of the taps. If the water supply is cut off for a day or so, we can rely on the state to help us get water back into our bodies to keep going. For occupied peoples in Palestine, a water shortage might be the beginning of the end. Many conflicts in Palestine result in severe water shortages and sewage overflows because of damage to the water and sanitation infrastructure. Palestinians have been waiting for decades for Israel to deliver on its promises to restore access to clean water in their homeland, but little happens.

Besides thirsting for water merely to survive and risking being attacked for trying to obtain water, Palestinians also endure occasional Israeli Defense Forces "visits." I remember staying at a friend's place one night on the outskirts of Tulkarem, when I woke to the sound of the Israeli Defense Forces talking over CB radio outside our house. There is a constant awareness among Palestinians that the Israeli military is checking up on them, looking into their lives, and intimidating people with their presence.

My efforts to attend daily prayers seemed to inspire my other roommate, Muhammad, who decided to join me at the masjid to pray and to talk to some of the elders. We prayed in the Masjid al-Aqsa, which had opened recently after reconstruction, and also at the Masjid al-Marwani, another place of worship built on Haram esh-Sharif. Muhammad said he had not prayed for years, which shocked me. I was from the West and had come to Jerusalem, the City of Peace, to seek out religion. I was moved when he joined me in prayer.

One day outside the masjid, I heard a tour guide telling a group of Western tourists about the impact the occupation had had on the lives of Palestinians. He spoke with authority and obvious knowledge, and I could not stop myself from following him around so I could hear more. At the end of the tour, I introduced myself to the guide, a man by the name of Ali Jiddah. During the tour, he had spoken openly about his involvement in the PFLP, the Popular Front for the Liberation of Palestine, and acknowledged that he had spent seventeen years in prison for bombing Israeli targets in 1968. I was struck by his continued dedication to the cause despite the many hardships he'd suffered.

When we parted, Ali gave me his business card. I kept his card close to me at all times while I was in Jerusalem. Maybe it was naïve of me, but I thought that it might offer me some protection if I were stopped on the streets. If people saw I knew Ali Jiddah and was willing to call him to vouch for me, they might think twice about arresting me, or prevent them from thinking I was a spy. I considered his card an informal a passport into this locked-down city of Jerusalem.

On my way home, I retraced parts of the route Ali Jiddah had taken during his tour. This time, I looked at things differently. I noticed the stark contrast between the spacious homes in the Jewish quarter of West Jerusalem and the cramped living spaces in the Muslim and Christian parts of the city. When I stopped to buy something to eat, I asked the shopkeeper how he felt about the Jewish homes in the Muslim quarter that openly displayed the Israeli flag. "It is illegal to put even a picture of Arafat in front of our homes," the shopkeeper replied. "In Jerusalem, there are also cameras everywhere, and every move you make can be recorded."

I told him that kind of thing was an issue in the West because of human rights. He just looked at me and replied, "I see you are from a very different place."

In the street, I could see some kids playing in the street. *Will they grow up to struggle like Ali?* I wondered. One young boy looked exactly like my brother Omar. I finished my food and went over to the boy. I asked him what his name was.

"Adnan," he said. He kept asking me questions: Who was I? Where was I from? Was I a spy? He tugged at my heart, for he was just as curious as Omar had been as a young boy. Sadly, Omar had got caught up in Edmonton's gang life and was struggling. I felt homesick. I could not help Omar get his life back on track, but I could give Adnan something to engage his mind. When I left, I gave Adnan some money, which he took. I saw Adnan often after that, and each time we chatted. He took an interest in my camera and wanted to know how it worked, so showed him and let him carry it around for me as I made my way through the city. That way, he could earn the money I gave him.

There were posters on the walls of a masjid that had been shut down by the Israelis. "Up with the Intifada!" the writing on one of the posters screamed. It showed a boy whose hand could barely hold the rock he is about to throw. And I thought of Ali Jiddah's children, the ones who loved to draw but drew only what they saw in the streets of the Old City. Ali had told us about the clashes between the police and Muslims who wanted to pray at a local masjid. At home in Canada, we had our troubles, but no one had ever shut down our mosque. The shopkeeper was right: I was now in a different place.

14

Chaos at Masjid al-Aqsa

Bearing witness to history can be dangerous and terrifying. It was Thursday, 28 September 2000, the day the hardline Zionist candidate Ariel Sharon was coming to visit the Masjid al-Aqsa. This part of the Old City is filled with ancient stone walls, narrow alleyways, and arches. Over the past few weeks, I had been taking photos, and here, I took a few more. When I developed the pictures and reviewed some of them, I could see and feel the tension and the power dynamics between the Israelis and Palestinians. In one picture, Israeli horses and police officers with tinted one-way sunglasses overpower Palestinian protesters. The power dynamics between victim and aggressor is clearly illustrated.

It seemed that the troops had multiplied in preparation for Sharon's visit—there were hundreds of them standing on top of crumbling buildings and filling the streets. More than anything else, their presence indicated that Ariel Sharon, a former Israeli defense minister who had overseen the massacre of thousands of Palestinians, knew exactly what symbolic power was attached to the timing of his visit, and that he understood well how he stood to gain politically from provoking the Palestinians. The following day, 29 September, would mark Rosh Hashanah, the start of the Jewish new year, which was a significant event for Orthodox Jews. The Likud Party that he had founded with another former prime minister and minister of defence, Menachem Begin, relied on the support of these hardline conservative voters, and he knew that visiting the Masjid al-Aqsa would be a show of force that would solidify their support for his party. He undoubtedly also knew that 2 October marked the start of Rajab, one of the four sacred months in Islam during which battles are prohibited, except in self-defence. The name of the month means "respect," but it can also signal veneration, or fear and awe of God. Ariel Sharon wanted to make Palestinians fear and respect him, as if he were a god. The presence of heavily armed soldiers and police just before a month in which Muslims are to live peacefully was a deliberate provocation that emphasized "fear and awe" and contradicted his stated mission of peace.

I met Adnan outside the gates of the Old City. From there, we walked towards the Lion's Gate, one of the main gates of Jerusalem, together. As we approached the Gate, I saw several journalists—one from Reuters news service, two Arabs, an Israeli, and one freelancer. They were all denied entry, even the Israeli. Having seen what was happening to the other journalists who had cameras with them, I was certain I would be denied entry as well. Fortunately, Adnan was quick and sharp and assessed the situation in an instant. He rushed up to me and took the camera. He quickly shot some photos of the action, and even managed to get me in some of the shots. I was glad that he had taken the initiative. Even if I couldn't get further than this, I now had evidence to show my father, Uncle Yazan, Uncle Faisal and others back home that I had been there and wasn't just showing them pictures that any tourist might have taken.

Some soldiers in a big blue van called Adnan and me over and frisked us. I was carrying my school bag. As one of the soldiers took it, he asked me, "What are you doing here? Why are you here?"

In that moment, I was terrified. There was too much happening and could not process it all. I wondered whether I too would be turned away like the Palestinians, or whether they would let me go. As scared as I was, I also did not want to sell out my people. I thought about how I had done that when I told people my name was Moe because I was embarrassed by my Arabic heritage. This time, I wanted to acknowledge my heritage. If anyone had a right to be afraid in this situation, it was Adnan and the other Palestinian youth. They knew these soldiers and they knew what they could and could not do, yet there Adnan was beside me, defiant as ever.

"I am a Canadian visiting Palestine, learning about my Palestinian heritage and teaching English at Al-Quds University," I said when the soldiers asked me what I was doing there.

The Israeli soldier tried to speak to me in very broken Arabic, but I could not understand him, so I asked, "Can you speak English to me?"

Another soldier came up and stared at me. "Have you ever been to prison?"

I laughed and pointed to the passport his partner was holding. "You've got my passport. You can see I am Canadian. If I had been in prison, I probably wouldn't be here now. Why do you ask?"

The soldier stared at me in silence for a while before waving me and Adnan through. They let me go. Lucky, unlucky, lucky—it was a game of chance. I must be many times blessed.

Slowly, we made our way towards the masjid with the crowd. As we approached Al-Aqsa, I could see Ali Jiddah. He couldn't stop himself from being where the action was. All around me, the noise of conversation—in Hebrew, Arabic, English—was getting louder and more agitated.

Even if I wanted to enter the masjid, the was no chance of that happening. Right in front of me stood the biggest man I'd ever seen in my life, an Israeli soldier all dressed in black. I'm six foot two, but he was about five inches taller and around 350 pounds, solidly built and holding an assault rifle. As I moved away, the tension around me unravelled into chaos.

As Sharon arrived at the Masjid al-Aqsa, some people rushed up to the security line and started to throw stones, but the Israeli soldiers and bodyguards held tight. The crowd yelled at Sharon, shouting for him to stop the "instigating" and get out of the sacred Masjid al-Aqsa. Soldiers were shooting rubber bullets at the demonstrators. They were supposedly non-lethal bullets, but I knew enough to know that these "kinetic impact munitions" can cause bone fractures, internal-organ injury, permanent disability, and even death.

I saw two men being quickly bandaged up, the heavy gauze hanging limp in the air before it was wrapped tightly around their wounds, and then returning to the line. I saw an old man being clubbed on the head by a soldier. I could hear it crack on the man's skull, it was so close. Amid the swinging clubs, the blood, the falling, people began to shout "Allahu Akbar!" Even in this wild scene, they were not yelling things like "Death to Israelis!" or "Die, stupid enemy!"—they just confirmed their allegiance to God. The phrase literally means "God is great!" and is used as a shocked expression or invocation, like saying "Oh my God!" The expression is also used to symbolize that fact that even though Palestinians are weaker now, we have God on our side. If we are overpowered by Israeli weapon-power, we will invoke the greatness of God who is bigger and larger than anyone to take back our rights. But here, in the midst of the protest, it sounded like a battle cry, and I knew how it would be misinterpreted on television.

Somewhere in the crowd, I could hear Ali Jiddah joining in with his strong voice, keeping others going when they were short of breath. I found myself saying "Allahu Akbar!" too, for only God could intervene in this chaos. Men and youths with rocks, chairs, and garbage cans—even school kids with backpacks and bags stuffed with books—were scrambling to find stones to throw. And around us the Israeli police were letting loose with rubber bullets and tear gas.

The screaming was getting more personal. "Murderer, murderer!" the Palestinians shouted and chanted, some of them pursuing Sharon down the Haram esh-Sharif.

"We will redeem the Haram with blood and fire!"

"Take that, take that—for Sabra and Shatila!"

On the other side, some Orthodox Jews were screaming, "Go back to Mecca!"

I could feel my asthma kicking in, so I pulled back. I covered my nose and mouth, but even so, I felt the asthma getting worse. I reached into my bag and pulled out my inhaler. I watched the events unfold from a distance while I waited for the medication to kick in. I could see two Israeli policemen being rushed away on stretchers. Nearby, Palestinian officials were protesting loudly about how they had been beaten on the head by police officers.

Abdulmalik Dahamshe, an Israel-Arab MP, joined the chanting crowd. "All the time Sharon wants to see more blood, more killing," Dahamshe shouted.

My asthma felt more under control, so I rejoined the crowd. As we moved away from the masjid, my heart was pounding. More scuffles broke out between Jews and Arabs, and more soldiers were arriving to break up the fighting.

People seemed to know they could not keep it up, not here, not today. The demonstration fizzled out. Things died down.

I found Adnan and got my camera back. We made our way to the city gates and left the Old City smouldering with tires and emotion behind.

When I left Edmonton, feeling the strong hugs of my family, I hadn't expected to find myself in what would be called "the worst violence here for several years" on the news. Was it just a day of commotion, with some awful injuries, my asthma going overtime, and then everyone going back to their places? I walked around outside the Old City, looking for an Internet café where I could sit down and let the adrenalin work its way out of my body as I wrote down my thoughts.

15

Violence in the Streets

It was Friday, a day of prayer, the day after Sharon's appearance at Masjid al-Aqsa. Almost twenty thousand Muslims had gathered at the masjid for dawn prayers, and with them came the rows of police officers. They were clearly there to intimidate the faithful after the events of the previous day.

I was still on the bus to Jerusalem, hoping to be at the masjid for *dhuhr* prayer time at noon when news began to filter through to us over the radio. As people hopped onto the microbus, they relayed what they had heard: The demonstrations began right after prayers. Youth were throwing rocks as if their lives depended on it—because their lives *do* depend on this struggle. When the police could no longer handle the barrage of angry youth, the soldiers in full riot gear came in and started shooting at people, live ammunition as well as rubber bullets. The Palestinian Authority had spoken up. On its official radio station, the Voice of Palestine, it had called on "all Palestinians to come and defend Al-Aqsa." Even though Palestinians often sneered at the PA because they felt the organization was only serving its own interests and working with Israel to undermine Palestinian interests, people listened. Schools were closed and students arrived at the Haram esh-Sharif in buses. Speakers were blasting Arabic beats, almost always including Ahmad Kaabour's greatest hit, "Ounadikom," which had recently been re-released.

When I had stood outside Edmonton's Al-Rashid Mosque with my pellet gun as a thirteen-year-old almost exactly a decade before, I had thought that I might die and had wondered why a mere child should be made to carry a weapon. Now I was on a bus, headed into a battlefield armed only with my curiosity, but I was beginning to understand the questions a naïve young boy in Edmonton could not answer.

Wael, Muhammad and Ali had warned me not to go into the city for prayers, but rather to go to a local masjid in Abu Dis, but I imagined I could use my Canadian passport to get me through blockades and out of trouble if necessary. The bus driver dropped us off as close to the Old City as he could get, and I walked the rest of the way. I was in the thick of things now, surrounded by real heroes—people who faced real bullets. This time, I was not a child standing outside the mosque with a pellet gun mired in self-pity. I could smell the fear, feel it, hear it. It could sense the tension, the courage, and the hesitation. I was tense, scared, and excited. I was finally living the stories I had only heard from others or had read about.

A bullet pinged by my leg. It frightened me and I felt a nauseating rush in my body. This was really happening. Then the action fell into sequence. I could feel my body dissociating from the events and it felt as though I was watching the day unfold in a movie. Detaching myself from the here and now was the only way I could cope with the trauma I was experiencing. I wondered whether I would die a martyr, or whether I would be a spectator only. I was confused, worried, excited, scared. Amid the chaos that was unfolding round me at Al-Aqsa, as I was gasping for breath, I thought, *Dad, I love you. I love you and I don't know how you made it. I never knew what it was like for you and the others. If I die, Dad, Mom, will you be happy I am a martyr?*

Two more bullets flew by near my head. I shook myself. I didn't have to die now. I should be as smart as those kids hiding behind the trees. I could see things slamming against the trunks. There were sounds—crackling, spattering, whining, and popping. Not rocks. I was only a hundred metres away from the soldiers, and I could see plainly that they were firing at people indiscriminately—men, women, children, it did not matter to them. And even as the bullets headed one way, rocks were going the opposite direction. It was raining rocks, hundreds of them, big and small, flying with speed and force that didn't seem possible. They were hitting the riot police shields, drumming into them, and bouncing off like hail. Bullets continued to whizz by in response.

When I had caused trouble in Edmonton, I could predict possible outcomes and could assess the risks, but here it was different. I had arrived in the Old City wanting to be part of the action, but I quickly realized I was out of my depth. Instead of joining the protesters, I stood on the sidelines and turned to doing what I knew, which was taking videos. As much as I would have loved to be part of the action, I knew that what I could contribute was to create a video record. In the frenzy of the moment, I tried to get my video camera to work so that I could film what I was seeing. It did not help that I could see the *Musta'ribeen*—the Israeli soldiers that look Arabic and speak Arabic—joining the protesters and egging them on. Then in a split second they would pull black masks over their heads and start arresting protesters.

The crowd kept pushing towards Qubbat as-Sakhra, the Dome of the Rock, cornering the blue uniformed riot police who were stationed at the gates. They started firing rubber bullets at the crowd as they retreated. As they retreated, the green uniforms of the Israeli Defense Forces started to join them, running from the gate closest to Qubbat as-Sakhra. Their weapons weighed heavily on their bodies. I could hear the sound of the gunfire change with their arrival. They were shooting live rounds! Unlike the riot police who fired shots into the ground, the IDF soldiers were aiming directly at the crowd. They were aiming to kill.

The riot police, emboldened by the presence of the IDF, began to push forward again. Now, their fire became more focused, deliberate. This time, there was live ammunition as well as rubber bullets. I knew they were live bullets because people stopped throwing stones and turned to run away when the soldiers dressed in green started to shoot indiscriminately into the crowd. People fell and some did not get back up. With rubber bullets, people got back up and pushed closer. They were not doing that now. Also, there was more blood as the live bullets struck people and exploded.

As I ran for cover under fire of the bullets, I saw people being hit in the legs and in the head. One youth was struck in the forehead. He died instantly. Blood spouted from his head as demonstrators fled. Those who couldn't get out of the Qubbat as-Sakhra complex clung to the shadow and sanctuary of the masjid, but they couldn't escape the bullets. I saw blood everywhere. Another bullet flew past. A man died in front of me, three metres away.

I moved along with the crowd. Just outside the masjid, I heard someone yell, "Hey! You!"

I jumped. It was an Arab youth, one of a group who had positioned themselves at the entrance to the masjid to check that no *Musta'ribeen* were trying to enter. I could see from their faces that they were prepared to hurt anyone who tried to stop the rioters or the people throwing stones from the rooftops. He continued to shout at me in Arabic, fear and anger twisting his face into a grin.

"Where are you from? What are you?"

I began answering him, talking very fast.

"Your Arabic," he said, "it sounds foreign."

UNDER THE NAKBA TREE

I couldn't believe it. In this hell, he was criticizing the way I spoke. He had others with him. I thought they were going to kill me. I found myself scrambling in my pocket and bag. "Here, man, look at my Canadian passport.. I'm not Israeli. I have an Arab name."

While the youth was interrogating me, I caught sight of Adnan among the crowd outside the premises. I shoved the camera into his hands and told him to shoot videos of me, just like he had the day before.

"It's okay," said the youth at the checkpoint. "If you don't have weapons, go and find cover, and don't be some idiot from Canada."

I wanted to find shelter more than anything else at that moment, but I was fighting my way through a cloud of tear gas, and unable to get out. The allegedly non-lethal gas ripped into my nose and eyes and tore through my mouth and lungs as I struggled to breathe. I felt an asthma attack closing in on me again, just like the day before. I needed to close my stinging eyes. I was blinded.

I managed to crouch behind a wall. In the chaos, I'd lost sight of Adnan. I gulped and wheezed, fighting the tear gas. I remembered how, as students, we joked about the information that was printed by the university to manage risk from usually peaceful rallies on campus: *If you are in a crowd that is being dispersed involuntarily by the police, it is important to leave in larger groups so that you will have witnesses and support. Some tactics used by police are pepper spray, tear gas, etc.* Right now, I thought, I could use a support group to get me out of here. What I knew about tear gas came from student information sessions and pamphlets. Its effects wear off quickly, the pamphlets said. It wasn't just babies and old people who could suffer more permanent damage. What they didn't tell you, or what I couldn't remember, was how to stop the searing pain.

≪ · ≫

I don't know where it came from, but all of a sudden, like a blessing, there it was—a long piece of cloth stuffed into my hand. I was still trying to be an international observer, looking out from my refuge with tear-streaked eyes as I was wheezed and choked—and this scarf came to my rescue out of nowhere. I slapped it against my face and tied it behind my head. This was not Dickinsfield High in Edmonton, where I had put on a show with a misunderstood scarf. This keffiyeh was a lifeline.

In 1987, during the First Intifada, I was just beginning to understand what being Palestinian meant. I was only ten years old, and in Canada, when the Palestinian uprising erupted in the Israeli-occupied territories. It began with violence and fighting as intense as in 1948 and 1967. Whenever I heard about it, in bits and pieces, it was from my family or other adults. They had come to Canada for a better, safer future. By 1993, the sixth year of the First Intifada, it seemed the Palestinians had at last received some recognition and respect from the Western world—but there was little from Israel, and no commitments for change. Now, in this moment, as I crouched behind a wall in Old Jerusalem, I did not think of myself as Canadian. Yes, I had grown up and had lived there most of my life, but right then I felt as if Palestine had been my lifelong home. I felt the loss of loved ones more closely than ever before and could imagine having had my home bulldozed. I felt that I personally had been suspected, arrested, and tortured and was always watched, taunted, and targeted. In that moment, it was as though I had lived for years under Israeli occupation, trying to keep the family together, seeing violence many days in the year, hearing about wars and demonstrations. A citizen of nowhere, someone who knew only occupation.

When people experience the barrage of injustices as Palestinians have endured for generations, they will double their efforts to achieve justice for themselves and their children.

Being victimized generation after generation was not making Palestinians cower. On the contrary, that was what made my people a threat to Israel. In this moment, I realized, I was witness to the crimes committed against us, and as my breathing eased under the keffiyeh, I thought how our survival incriminated our oppressors.

I'd first seen the Palestinian flag—red, green, black, and white—at home in Canada, in a parade. There it was simply a flag, a symbol of identity among many others. Here, every time the Palestinian flag was raised, bullets were fired. At one point, I could hear a man shouting over the loudspeakers about a massacre, calling for ambulances. Back home, I had heard about massacres in Palestine. Now I was in the middle of one.

How quickly would the ambulances get here? How efficient would things be? I thought of my eye injury as a child and being rushed to hospital by my father, driving like a madman, the police helping us get there even faster. That was not going to happen. Not here. Not today.

Children were running behind cars, their feet pounding, raising clouds of dust, some trying to use slingshots, their hands frantic and angry. They were like any guerrilla army, working with the little they had. I saw makeshift weapons thrown at their targets, bottles smashing, gas igniting into a blossom of fire. I couldn't believe these children, how brave and brazen they were. One of them, about thirteen years old, was being beaten by grown men. Not far from that horror, I came across a woman in her sixties, wearing her traditional embroidered Palestinian abaya and a white hijab. She had a wound on her leg but was still cursing the soldiers as she threw the stones that other women were collecting for her. I don't know which was more terrible, the look on her face or the wound in her leg. Seeing her power reminded me of the strength of Palestinian Muslim women—the strength of my mother, who walked through dark city streets putting up her Herbalife® posters to generate income as a single mother of five children. In her own way, my mother was fighting to preserve her culture and religion in Canada, and I knew she would have been formidable here in Palestine.

Many of the Israeli soldiers on that terrifying day in September 2000 looked younger than me, perhaps eighteen or nineteen. They did not look like a formidable Israeli force. Surrounded by an angry mob throwing rocks at them, they simply looked frightened. I struggled to understand why they were so frightened fighting civilians who were mostly throwing rocks at live machine-gun fire.

The live ammunition kept coming, and people kept running and crawling through the gates. As we ran outside the gates, I heard the thud of Israeli clubs falling on the heads and backs of people behind me. Most of the people at the back of the crowd were women, both young and old. A woman fell down in front of me, but no one could get to her—there was too much chaos. As I saw her disappear under the feet of a fleeing crowd, I felt the oppression and the pain, my parents carried.

The loudspeaker put out a call that hospitals were looking for blood donors to help treat the wounded. Muhammad and I decided to find a servees that could take us to the Makassed hospital, which was the closest and easiest to get to from the Qubbat as-Sakhra. It was the one concrete thing I felt do to help. Every step Muhammad and I took away from Al-Aqsa seemed to lead us into further protests. Both Ehud Barak and Yasser Arafat were fools if they thought they could stop things now. It was madness—in some places, it was action that didn't end.

How quickly the children I'd seen on the streets in the days before had become warriors. Children! Just the age I'd been while trying to discover where I belonged in Edmonton. They had set up checkpoints on the periphery of the Old City and looked more like adults than I had when I had defended Al-Rashid Mosque against vandals and violence. If I couldn't stand up outside a mosque for more than one night, what would I have been like at a checkpoint?

As we arrived at the hospital, we saw soldiers on top of the hill and demonstrators at the bottom. Some of the protesters had the keffiyeh wrapped around their face and neck—to prevent having themselves and their families recognized and targeted by Israeli forces. I had pulled mine off my face and used it to wipe off the sweat and dust. If my asthma got worse, I could surely get help at the hospital. Muhammad and I laughed nervously about that. The emergency rooms were filling up with the crushed and bloody humans being carried and pulled through the crowd—rushing to be treated at a backlogged, undersupplied hospital or to be wrapped in an outlawed flag as a funeral shroud. We doubted that an asthma attack would be considered an emergency.

As a Muslim and Arab in the West, I've had my own kind of suffering, and no doubt others who have immigrated to North America or who were born there will understand. Those who had always been here in the Middle East might have doubted me if I had told them that Canadian officers, such as members of the settler-serving RCMP or Constable Case Model from the Edmonton Police Service, had some things in common with the Israeli forces.

In the end, my efforts to get to one of the hospitals came to nothing. Even though I had donated blood in Canada, they would not accept my blood in Jerusalem, not even on a day when the Palestinian blood that flowed in my veins was being spilled not far from me. They said it was because I had asthma, but I found that hard to believe, as it had not prevented me from donating blood in Canada. There was no direct transport back to Abu Dis, which meant that we first had to go back the Old City to get a ride home. On the way back from the hospital, I again saw the elderly woman who had been throwing stones during the protests. She was still wearing her traditional embroidered abaya and was walking along, despite her wound. The man driving our vehicle was not slowing down, but I told him, "No, stop . . . pick her up. She is an old woman and deserves respect." To me, this woman was a revolutionary; she brought tears to my eyes. The driver stopped. When we arrived at a checkpoint, the driver was tense, because he thought the kids there might begin throwing rocks at his bus. It certainly looked as though they might. The woman opened her window and yelled at them. It was like their mother or grandmother screaming at them. Embarrassed, they stopped what they were doing, and let our bus pass undisturbed. It was almost humorous.

The servees driver stopped a little way from the gates and the old woman and I walked the rest of the way to the Old City. "I have been shot twice," she said as we went through the gate, "But every time they hit me, I come back stronger."

16

Family Ties

The old woman and I parted company just beyond the gates—
she went home, and I caught a servees back to Abu Dis. Safely
back home after a full day at Al-Aqsa and then the hospital,
Muhammad and I turned the dial on the radio until we found
the Voice of Palestine radio station. I felt a strange sense of relief
coming off the adrenalin. My eyes were no longer weeping uncon-
trollably, but they did feel scratchy from the chemicals. It would
take a few days for my throat and lungs to stop burning. The
announcer was calling events of the day "The Battle of Jerusalem."
The battle had followed the riots of Thursday, 28 September, when
the tension that had built up around the circumstances of occupation was stoked and channelled by Ariel Sharon, his colleagues,
and the armed Israeli officers. Hanan Ashrawi, a Palestinian
legislator, scholar, and human rights activist, blamed the Israelis
for a "massacre" against the Palestinians, describing their actions
as deliberately "targeting peaceful worshippers" rather than per-
petuating "random violence." I thought of how Palestinians were
portrayed in the news in North America. So often, we were represented simply as Arab troublemakers. During my conversations
with people I met, and from reading the papers and listening to

the news, I learned that a hundred thousand people had showed up in solidarity at a rally in Washington to protest Israeli occupation, oppression, and the destruction of Palestine. I wondered what the Canadian newspapers were saying, as I had not seen any mention of Canada's response to the crisis.

When I heard Israeli prime minister Ehud Barak on the radio saying he hoped these incidents "wouldn't affect the peace process" and that parties seeking peace should "stop fighting now," I felt a desire to talk to someone like Uncle Yazan back home—someone who could help me understand all the thoughts and feelings that flew through my head like bullets. Perhaps between the two of us we could figure out why Barak would say the things he was saying—he had, after all, approved Sharon's visit to Haram esh-Sharif. And anyway, how could people stop fighting just like that?

Pretending, hoping, that life would have returned to normal, I went to Al-Quds first thing on Saturday morning. Muhammad came with me. I picked up a newspaper on my way to the bus stop. No city buses were entering Abu Dis, so I had to use a servees. On the way into the city, the driver stopped to pick up a man.

"What's the situation like in Jerusalem," he asked as he boarded the bus.

"Bullets flying, people dying," was the driver's response.

A youth seated in front of us turned around. "Normal," he said.

To me, the man was describing a place of carnage; for the children who grew up here, it was the status quo. In Edmonton, someone getting on the bus might talk about the weather. Here, you asked about people's safety, hoping to find out how strict the Israelis were being as they forced their control over Palestinians.

Muhammad and I read the paper and listened to the radio on the way in. Ramallah, Beit Lahm, Tulkarem, Gaza, Nablus— all were on fire. When we drove close to the police checkpoint just outside the Old City, Muhammad asked the driver of the servees to stop. He did not want to face the Israeli officers. But I told him to keep driving. He stopped at the checkpoint. The officers checked our documentation, then let us pass. How different it felt from the previous day, when children had set up and staffed the checkpoints going out of the Old City.

Al-Quds was ghostlike and littered with rubble from the previous day. There were Israeli soldiers everywhere. Burned-out tires lay smouldering in the streets. They had been rolled into the street as a way to block the soldier's view when the police fired on protesters—a toxic but ingenuous way for protesters to protect themselves. I was noticing everything, soaking it up. Breathing it in. It stung.

All the shops were closed, either in protest or as a sign of respect for those who had been killed in the conflict. To soothe the trauma of the day, we decided we needed some real Palestinian food. We found a man barbecuing some kebabs on the street. Muhammad and I stood amid the carnage, listening to the sizzle of the meat, watching the smoke from his grill rising into the air. We watched with admiration as he carefully turned the kebabs loaded with vegetables.

As I took in the devastation and ate my kebab, the news about Ramallah gnawed at me. I had family there and I wanted to see for myself what the situation was like for them, so Muhammad and I found a servees to take us there.

Along the way, we passed through several Palestinian Authority checkpoints without incident, much to Muhammad's relief. We got to the outskirts of Ramallah around mid-morning and pulled up at another checkpoint. As we got off the bus while the authorities checked the vehicle, I made the mistake of point-ing my camera at the ambulances and the PA officers. A PA soldier approached and asked what I was doing.

"Just observing," I told him.

"Are you a reporter?" he said.

"Freelance."

"Come and meet my superior."

I think our driver must've known what was coming, because he drove off as soon as the PA authorities started speaking to us. The officer asked for my passport. I gave it to him, and Muhammad also handed over his ID. I always felt a twinge of dis-comfort when I saw my passport leave my hands and end up in the hands of strangers who could do anything they wanted with it.

In the superior's office, we were asked a few questions, our bags were confiscated, and we were ordered to go and wait in the back of their Jeep. After a while, I was told I could leave but had to come back in the morning for questioning. Muhammad had to stay, they said.

I refused to leave without my friend. "No, I will go for ques-tioning now," I said.

The officer shrugged. He didn't seem concerned either way. "The reason we are detaining you," he said as we walked back to the office, "is because the Israeli soldiers are using camcorders and filming people so they are later investigated—and you have a camcorder."

"You think I am Israeli?"

The man shrugged. "Sometimes it is difficult to tell."

I couldn't help but laugh wryly. I was learning that even here people saw me as different and had trouble accepting me for who I am. In Canada, white Canadians often asked me where I was from, as if I saying I was from Edmonton was not enough. But it felt dif-ferent somehow when a Palestinian doubted where I was from.

In a reversal of my fortunes, Muhammad now was free to go, and I had to stay. I told him to leave, but he wouldn't. I threatened to make a big scene if he did not leave, but he stubbornly insisted that he would not abandon me. So they detained him as well.

There we were, detained in one of the PA centres, confined by conflict and my desire to document this mayhem. As we walked in, the officers asked if we were hungry. We said yes and they brought us a plateful of *bamiyeh* with rice. As we ate, we sat and watched television reports of men and women being killed or finding their way to the hospital. The detention space was like a coffee shop, with no formalities—in fact, the whole thing seemed *househ*—confused and disorganized.

We were asked questions in an intelligence agency building called the *Mukhabarat*, which means Intelligence. When we were done, we were told we were free to leave. As we walked thought the front office the officer there said, "Don't use your camcorder. The Palestinian authorities might imprison you for a month or so."

We thanked him for the advice and left. As immersed as I was I the unfolding events, I realized, I remained a foreigner. They did not offer us a ride back downtown, so we found another servees to take us into the city. We wanted to be there because we had seen on the television that there was open conflict on the edges of Ramallah, and we thought it might be safer downtown. As we drove into the city, we could see the Israeli soldiers firing at children who were throwing rocks. Beyond them, about 750 metres down the hill, I could see a hotel with some Israeli soldiers standing on the roof, shooting down at the protesters. I asked a nearby PA officer if I could use my camcorder.

"Go ahead," he said, "but don't film people at close range and don't get too close to the hotel—too many snipers."

It was chaotic. People were throwing rocks at police and soldiers stationed on the ground. Tear gas smoke clung to the air and bullets were flying everywhere. Around me, the wounded fell to the ground. There they sat. Those who could took cover, holding onto their stomachs, legs, or arms—whatever part of their body was injured.

Up against a wall, I heard bullets pinging close to my head—once, twice, three times. Fragments of cinderblock flew into my face. I scrambled to the ground. A man nearby was shot in the leg.

There was destruction was everywhere—tires on cars had been shot out, people were dying around me. A man in front of me was arguing with Israelis and getting beaten right in front of me. I thought of the man who had died in front of me in Al-Quds the day before. I had been standing right there with my camcorder. Even if I could've acted in time to film his death, I didn't know if it was better to record the action, or to respect his moment of passing. I didn't know whether I could stomach a repeat of that experience less than twenty-four hours later.

When the crossfire of bullets and stones settled down a bit, we left downtown Ramallah and headed back to Muhammad and Wael's place in Abu Dis. It was a mess everywhere as we drove home. My fingers were itching to take out my camcorder. The driver could tell what I was thinking. "No—don't do it! It's trouble!"

On the radio in the servees, we heard that the man who had been shot in the head in Jerusalem was from Abu Dis. He was proclaimed a *shaheed*—a witness, a martyr.

In the past two days, I had seen the world as I knew it before shatter. As the news drifted over the airwaves, it dawned on me that I had witnessed the making of a martyr. A few feet to one side, and it could have been me.

About a week after my trip to Ramallah, my cousin Reham and her husband, Youssef, invited me to visit for a couple of days. When my family lived in Jordan, Reham's family lived next door and we visited all the time. In the middle of an exploding world, they invited me to come and visit. A normal invitation, as if nothing unusual was happening. "Hey, Mowafa, come and eat with us, come and stay over. You're family." I longed for such a sense of normality.

Reham and Youssef did not tell me about the constant IDF assaults where they lived—bullets, tanks, and gunfire during the night. The noise woke me up. Reham and Youssef were sound asleep. It was like just another night to them.

Whenever I could, I used an online service to phone my dad; witnessing death compelled me to reach out. But our conversations were difficult. Every time, my father would say, "Come back here, come back. What are you doing there? Come back now." He always said the same thing: that it was dangerous in Palestine and that I'd be better off back in Canada with a steady job. I could not bring myself to tell him that several times I had nearly been killed, or that there was little to draw me back to Edmonton. My father was in an unstable relationship. My mother and brothers were in Vancouver, and I often felt unwelcome in my own homeland.

But I could tell him about Reham and Youssef and my visit to Hebron. I wanted to tell my family where I was and assure them that I was being hosted with care and hospitality in the Arab way. Reham and Youssef let me use their phone.

"I'm fine," I told my parents. "I am well fed, and I have a good place to stay in Abu Dis, but last night was noisy." I couldn't bring myself to tell them the noise was from the fighting.

My parents would have liked to be reunited with some of their family in Palestine. As it turned out, I was the missing link, the connector, and often in surprising ways. Sometimes, it seemed, God would guide me in the most unexpected ways. One morning in mid-October, I stopped a servees to go to Bethlehem, but the driver said he was going to Ramallah. I was getting used to people asking me where I was from, so when the driver asked, I had an answer ready.

"My family is from Lydda," I told him. We were still talking about Lydda and the fact that he was heading to Ramallah when the radio in the cab announced another funeral for a martyr, a member of the Al-Anati family. That was my mother's family! I wanted to pay my respects, so I dropped my plans of going to Bethlehem and instead asked the driver if he could take me to where the *azza* (funeral) would be. He said he would.

Maybe I shouldn't go, I thought, not knowing who this person was or what relation he had been to me. After all, the deceased was a distant relative, connected to me through my great-grandmother's second marriage. Still, I wanted to go.

In Ramallah, the cab driver asked around where the funeral was being held. Eventually, we found a child who said he knew where to go, but it turned out to be the wrong funeral. The whole city was grieving. Disoriented, I felt like an idiot, but the family was very friendly. They told me to walk two blocks to find the ceremony I was looking for. I knew everything would be okay. I walked into the place, a local youth club, and the first person I saw was Abu Khalid, my mother's uncle on her father's side. My mother's uncle! I knew his family from Jordan when we used to visit there; they were our neighbours. I was shocked at how close this martyr, the man being mourned, was to me. "I came all the way from Canada to pay my respects," I said to everyone. I was joking, but also serious.

People were staring at me, nodding and smiling, whispering to each other. I offered my condolences to everyone, and some even remembered and recognized me. They seemed surprised but happy to see me. I went along the row of people, shaking hands, and finally came to my mother's second uncle. We kissed and hugged, and he introduced me to the family, which was large: "From Canada . . . Mowafaq Househ, son of Hanan Ghnaim and Said Househ."

It felt so good. I had not known I would find them when I went to the Middle East, though I had some vague idea of where they were. It was a funeral, yet the mood was not sad. People talked as they normally did, and they were smiling. In Islam, we are taught that martyrs are not dead: they are alive even though we are not with them. The idea is to rejoice because they are now with Allah, safe and at peace.

While I was with my family in Ramallah to commemorate my mother's cousin's death, I went to pray in the nearby masjid. I will not forget that day. It was 12 October, and I recall having to clear debris off the floor before I could say my prayers because the Israeli soldiers had bombed the masjid. It was dark inside because the bombing had cut the electricity as well. That was also the day two Israeli undercover agents were lynched in Ramallah. At least I found some comfort in the knowledge that my mother's cousin, the late Emad Anati, who had been working with the Palestinian Authority, had died defending Ramallah and his family against the IDF—fighting against the oppressor for his homeland, family, and religion. I felt proud and began to understand what death is often like in the homeland. I began to compose a letter to my mother in my mind:

Dear Mother,

I met many people, though some not directly. I have met your uncle, Abu Khalid, and I even met your cousin Emad. He gave his life for Palestine.

17

Surrounded by Family in the Middle of a War

After I had offered my condolences to family in Ramallah and had prayed at the local masjid, I returned to Abu Dis. Wael and Muhammad had gone home to visit their families, so I was alone at home. In a way, I was glad to be alone because I needed the time alone to process recent events. When I got home, I discovered the power in our apartment had been turned off. To sit in the darkness with the power cut off, listening to the battery-powered radio and learning about events that are occurring outside your doorstep, is a surreal experience. There were no streetlights that could shine even a sliver of light into the apartment. I couldn't see my hand in front of my face until my eyes adjusted to the blackness. Whatever identity I had was stripped away, blacked out. Alone in the darkness, I replayed the memories of soldiers using rockets, tanks, machine guns, and bullets during protests. Now they were moving beyond the city centres, encroaching on the suburbs of Palestinian towns and refugee camps. The Israelis were shooting at houses, sparing no one.

On the radio, a Palestinian from Ain al-Hilweh refugee camp in Lebanon had called in and was crying on the phone, saying,

"I want to be with my Palestinian brothers and sisters . . . to help them." Would the Israeli soldiers enter Abu Dis at night? the caller asked. Would they assault the town? Were we all suspect here? Is this why the power had been shut down? To offer them the cover of complete darkness? Under the agreement of the 1995 Oslo Accord, Abu Dis was under joint Israeli and Palestinian control. This meant that in most of the city, the Palestinian Authority took care of civilian matters, while Israel was in control of security. Clearly, electricity was considered a matter of security, for the Jerusalem Electricity Power Company provided electricity, and power cuts to our part of the city were not uncommon. Israeli needs came first. Abu Dis overlooked the Haram esh-Sharif from near Jabal al-Zaytun, the Mount of Olives, so its proximity to Jerusalem made the city a contender for becoming the capital of a Palestinian state. Was it a target now? My mind whirled with questions in the darkness.

With the IDF patrolling the streets and shooting indiscriminately, everyone was staying home to protect themselves. I hoped things would calm down and that the Israelis would get the message that Palestinians would continue to fight for our freedom until our death.

The news reports were filled with accounts of conflicts between Israeli soldiers and Palestinians, and the Israeli prime minister, Ehud Barak, had asked the troops to withdraw, but people were still being killed and injured severely by his forces. Conflict was heating up, with the many Palestinians who lived inside Israel leading demonstrations against Israeli forces.

During the *azza* I had attended in Ramallah, I had met my family, one after another, all in mourning, yet defiant and proud that their family's blood had been spilled for the Palestinian struggle. One cousin had spent ten years in prison. He was arrested when he was sixteen for killing a collaborator and was sentenced to life imprisonment but was released after a decade in prison and several appeals to his sentence.

When I began meeting some of my own family and discovered that we had a martyr among us, the conflict had become personal, and I felt the effects of Israeli brutality even more. I realized that it could easily have been me who had died battling Israeli forces, defending Ramallah and working with the Palestinian Authority.

I went to bed in the dark with my head bursting with images and thoughts. I woke up in the middle of the night to the sound of gunfire. A truck with a blaring loudspeaker drove by our apartment: "Oh men of Abu Dis, come out and defend your town, the Israelis have invaded." I turned on my radio but couldn't find out anything to give me more information about what was happening outside. In this Israeli-controlled town, when Arab citizens were attacked by settlers, the Israeli state did not seem to consider this a matter of security, and so did nothing. Citizens had to defend themselves. I could hear people coming out on the rooftops and opening their windows to see what was going on. The commotion went on for three hours after the announcement of an invasion. Then, in the early hours of the morning, a minor invasion of mosquitoes began, and I knew I wouldn't be going back to sleep. I felt attacked and itchy all over. I got dressed and sat waiting for the sun to rise over Al-Quds and bathe the Qubbat as-Sakhra in gold.

Over the next few days, the violence continued in Jerusalem and Abu Dis, in Ramallah, in Hebron, everywhere I'd been and where I had family. Through it all, the family connections grew stronger. I returned to my cousin Reham's house in Hebron, where I was wrapped in the warmth of traditional greetings and hospitality. Reham's husband, Youssef, was a dentist. He was an intelligent man who had lived for nineteen years in the West, mostly in Romania. His father was the most welcoming and generous elder I met in Palestine. Every time I visited Reham and Youssef, the old man would take me to his tiny vineyard and give me fresh grapes off the vines. Many people found it hard to believe that I was here, that I had wanted to come and live among "honourable people," but Youssef's father was not one of them. Every time we spoke, he encouraged me to stay in Palestine.

<< · >>

I had an aunt who lived in Mukhayyam Balata, the refugee camp adjacent to Nablus in the northern West Bank. Aunt Huda was my mother's half-sister. She was very poor and had no relatives left in Palestine. Her children had left or were in prison. One of her children was killed by an Israeli soldier. As a result, Aunt Huda felt very isolated and lonely. She could not contain her excitement when I contacted her to ask if I could visit.

I travelled alone to Nablus, stopping off again in Ramallah on the way there. It was chaos. Settlers were throwing rocks at Palestinian cars, and the streets were littered with rocks and glass. Nablus was closed off. To get there, I had to hitch a ride with the locals, who would speed through the mountains and villages, taking irregular routes. They knew every nook and cranny of this land. I had little choice but to trust them with my life and simply be a stunned passenger. In some ways, I had been the daring one back home in Edmonton, sticking my neck out, taking risks, but it was nothing like this. Back then, I sometimes thought I could feel my spirit dying, but here it might be my body departing along with it.

I was not the only one trying to get into Nablus. Several of us crammed into in an old Mercedes bus. The driver took us through mountain villages and back roads. My fellow passengers feared that settlers would act against us and that we might be killed by a soldier in one of the helicopters that circled above. As we crept through the empty streets of a village that was under a twenty-four-hour curfew at the time, we were stopped by Israeli soldiers. They ordered us to get out of the car and demanded everyone's identification. "Where are you going?" they asked.

One man, Muhammad, who was about twenty, was asked whether he spoke Hebrew. "*Aní lo medabér ivrít*—No, I don't speak Hebrew," Muhammad replied, in Hebrew.

The soldier looked at him for a moment, turned away, then suddenly spun back around and slapped him across the head. Muhammad staggered from the force of the blow. The rest of us stood frozen to the ground, stunned and unable to rush forward to defend one of our own.

Muhammad's eyes looked shiny but stayed fixed on the soldier. A tear slowly formed in one eye and squeezed its way out. He fought back more tears and stood defiantly straight in the sun. The soldier stared back, and we thought he was about to hit Muhammad again when one of the other soldiers said to his colleague in Arabic, "*Khalas*." Enough.

Then they let us go. We got back into the car and started off again. We were all silent, a hundred unsaid things hanging over us. Finally, the old man next to me broke the silence. "Not to worry son, all your mistakes will be forgiven, to this day, for that slap you received." All of us then consoled and congratulated him.

Eventually, we got to Nablus. As soon as I sat down my troubles left me and I felt spoiled by the generosity my aunt extended to me. I did not want to sleep at her place because I knew that when Arabs have guests they have to buy and purchase a lot of things and I did not want to overburden Aunt Huda and her husband because they were poor. As the evening approached, I bid them farewell and found a hostel nearby where I could sleep the night. When I woke in the morning, my money was gone.

Fortunately, the person was an honourable thief with enough compassion to leave me money to get back home to Abu Dis.

I found a servees that was headed back to Jerusalem and settled into my seat. When we arrived in Ramallah, there were more helicopters overhead. As I listened to the radio, I began to understand why we had encountered helicopters on the way to Nablus. It all had to do with the two Israeli soldiers who had been killed. Israel was exacting revenge. Ehud Barak's government claimed that the soldiers had taken a wrong turn when entering Ramallah and had not seen the Palestinian checkpoint flags. Usually when Israeli soldiers were caught in Palestinian territories, they were returned, but this was during the height of the Intifada and the soldiers were lynched, set on fire, and dragged around the streets of Ramallah. Their death reflected the tensions of the time.

Above us, the Apache helicopters and airplanes continued to circle over Ramallah, dropping bombs on the city. The streets had erupted with violence, and the electricity was shut off, reminding us that the Israelis controlled everything—from roads to water and phone lines. I felt overwhelmed. I had just made my way back to Ramallah from Nablus by criss-crossing a maze of roads that ran through the fragments of land that made up Palestine. I kept hoping for the situation to improve, but things just seemed to get worse and worse. All around the vehicle, I could see buildings that had been attacked, and burned-out cars. When a house is destroyed—whether because tanks and helicopters in Beit Jala fired shots at it or because it was bulldozed in Hebron, so much more is lost than just the building. I had recently learned about one home that had been destroyed by a missile, killing the father, and seriously wounding his family. Just like that, the family's future had been shattered, and the children have to grow up without the guidance of their father. I felt that this same violence had taken part of my parents from me, that this home-destruction program had caused the stress that split them.

I thought of what my grandfather's home in Lydda had meant to him, how Uncle Faisal had worked hard to find a new home in Canada, how my mother and father had created a home for a growing family in Edmonton. A family home should be filled with pride as well as love, and the small objects that make memories, like family pictures, heirlooms, and images of the Qubbat as-Sakhra. These objects of memory would all be lost in the flames of Ramallah. The thought saddened me.

The roads from Ramallah to Jerusalem were closed, but I found a car and driver to take me back to the city through the back roads. We were stopped at one checkpoint, and I was asked for my passport, but we were allowed through. Back in Jerusalem, at the Internet café, I phoned my dad and my mom, relieved to be connecting with people I knew—people far away who were important to me. Both my parents begged me to come back, but all I could think as they spoke was, *I don't want to run away from war like the previous generation did.* I wanted to stick it out.

As I made my way back to Abu Dis, hitchhiking where I could find someone to take me part of the way, and walking the other stretches, I passed by soldiers without being asked for ID. This happened to me often, and at those times, it troubled me that I was allowed to move around with ease while innocent old men and women were stopped and checked.

The past few days had been filled with strange contrasts—from peacefully picking and eating grapes in my relatives' garden in Hebron to the chilling shock of nasty encounters with soldiers on the road, and nightly gunfire no matter where I found myself. The gunshots would start at around 7 p.m., and people would begin to close their shops, though some remained open, not seeming especially concerned. "How can you be so cool when the firing is so close?" I asked shopkeepers time and again.

And each time, they'd say something like, "Today is nothing. You should have seen yesterday. For the last two weeks, every night there were helicopter machine-gun attacks. It becomes the daily routine. People are used to it."

A day or two after returning from Nablus, I sat at my cousin Reem's place watching TV. The news broadcaster reported that eight Palestinians had been arrested in connection with the deaths of the two Israeli soldiers in Ramallah. But the report did not say how they were apprehended. It did not say anything about the hundred Palestinians who had been killed, or about the hundreds who had been injured. Either there were no arrests made for crimes like these, or the soldiers were given light sentences. Court proceedings, it seemed, were only formalities. Arabs living outside the area of conflict, like many in Iraq, were donating food, supplies, and equipment to provide relief for Palestinians. They had sent a legion of doctors to nearby Jordan to help the wounded who could make it out of occupied Palestine and across the border.

As Reem and I were eating, I told her how I'd sometimes go to a Western fast-food joint to soothe my homesickness. When I did that, every bite, every sip, every crunch reminded me of times in Canada, and I longed to be back there. I was craving fast food more than ever, I said to her. She understood: It was time for me to go home. I didn't want to lose my sanity here, and I sensed that it could happen.

I told Reem a story about the time Uncle Faisal and his family had gone to the McDonald's at Northgate Centre mall. Someone called them "fucking Pakis" and told them to "go back to your country." My Aunt Khadija had taken off her shoes, and ready to use them as weapons to defend her family from these hoodlums. Reem laughed.

When that incident occurred, Uncle Faisal had been in Canada for many years and was doing well. All his kids had been born there, but the honeymoon was over. They didn't look like white Canadians, so a "happy meal" experience meant being dished up a healthy dose of racism and bigotry on the side. And yet, even as I told the story, I knew that the racism we experienced in Canada was different and that many Palestinians would never have the luxury of living in a country like Canada.

As we spoke and watched television, I decided I could deal with being here for a bit longer. I had some strength, and I wanted to observe and record everything. For now, just having a burger and fries was a real treat. In those moments of homesickness, a taste of my "Canadian" culture meant dipping salty fries in puddles of ketchup.

SOUTH

الجنوب

18

Crossing Borders

In early December 2000, before returning to Canada, I travelled to Lebanon. My Israeli visa was going to expire before my departure for Canada, and the only way I could renew it was to leave the country and re-enter. This gave me a good excuse to look up a friend from Edmonton, Wassim—a brilliant anti-authoritarian who had become a successful businessman and was in Lebanon at the time. Although we had known each other in high school, we became close during my two-week visit to Lebanon, and remain so to this day. There was another reason, too. Uncle Yazan—who was encouraging me to stay, explore, and network—had sent a thousand dollars to Wassim, asking him to pass it on to me. I needed the money, but my pride prevented me from accepting it. In the end, Wassim said, "If you don't take it, I will burn it in front of you." I knew Wassim was serious about doing that and since Uncle Yazan had sent the money as a gift, I relented and accepted his generosity.

I took several servees taxis to get me from Palestine to Jordan, where I spent a few days with family. It was lovely to reconnect and share stories. Being in Palestine in the midst of all the violence had taken its toll on me, and I welcomed the break.

So, I am sure, did my parents, for they worried from a distance. Visiting family in Jordan would reassure them that I was safe and healthy. From Jordan, I took a taxi to Syria, and then found a ride that was headed to Saadnayel in the Beqaa Valley, which is where my family fled from during Black September, which is the name given to the 1971 conflict between the Kingdom of Jordan and the PLO under Yasser Arafat.

It was Ramadan, and the fertile beauty of the Beqaa Valley contrasted sharply with everything that had been happening around me, making me yearn for peace in the country of my people. We fasted from early morning to night, and I did not have to travel far to find a masjid. It was cooler now, since Ramadan began that year on the evening of Monday, 27 November, and ended on the evening of Thursday, 28 December.

Despite the support from Uncle Yazan, my money was running out. My sister back home was having a baby, my birthday was coming up, and the visa extension I'd arranged when I went to Lebanon was about to expire. I needed to return home to Canada. The three months I had spent in Palestine had exhausted me physically, and not even the short break in the Beqaa Valley could fix the weariness inside me. As I drove back from Lebanon, I thought about how this short time had affected me and wondered how people could face every day of their lives what I had endured for a short time and still survive.

As soon as I got back to Abu Dis, I started planning for my flight to Toronto. At the checkpoints on the way to the airport on the day of my departure, police and soldiers with guns were checking under the cars for bombs. As I made my way through Customs and Immigration, I set my bag down for a few seconds at one of the checkpoints. An officer quickly approached and told me not to do that.

"You are Canadian?" the security officer asked, even though that is what it said on my passport.

"Yes," I replied.

He looked up. "Where were you born?"

"Canada," I said. The tone of in the officer's voice put me on guard. I was ready to go home and did not want to get into any trouble. I had spent the last of my money and did not know what I would do if they didn't let me through.

"Where is your father from?" he asked.

"Palestine," I replied. It was the first time I had said that without hesitation, and it felt good.

While the officer had been asking me questions, another officer was looking through my luggage. When they had finished look at my bags, the office said, "We are going to strip-search you now."

I did not know what the law allowed Israeli officials to do, and I worried he might detain me and make me miss my flight. The officer and took me to a private room and made me remove all my clothing, except my underwear. He was very professional, but I will never forget that feeling of my body being thoroughly examined and invaded. It filled me with rage. *It took going home to Canada to understand what it was like to live in Palestine,* I thought during the flight home.

When the plane touched the ground in Toronto, I cried. It was as if I had just awakened from a nightmare and had realized that I am in a safe place among family. The nightmare was over. As I made may way to Customs and Immigration and into Canada, the war, the sad stories, and the checkpoint experiences flooded through my mind.

The passport officer stamped my passport.

"Welcome home," he said. A sense of relief washed over me as I walked away. It was not just relief at being home, but of knowing that I could now grieve without fear for my people who lived under occupation. I was back in a familiar zone, among people I could trust, and this trust came from the vision and protection of my parents, who had planned and worked to support the family for more than two decades. I knew that, in the 1960s, Uncle Faisal could not have foreseen our paths as he arrived in Canada—the first of many refugees in our family. Similarly, my grandmother had hoped to offer my father safety when she saved him from under the Nakba tree. What I was now feeling is what they dreamt of, and still dream of, for me—*Salaam*. Peace.

In Edmonton, I felt happy to be home and less preoccupied with day-to-day violence in a place where education and health care were within reach—unlike Palestine, where getting access to even basics is a struggle. And yet, I also felt uneasy in a place where I felt I did not fully belong. My father says Edmonton is his home, but it seldom felt like home to me. I was always wandering, searching for my physical and spiritual home. My time in Palestine had confirmed for me what I had experienced as a child growing up in Edmonton: for Palestinians, the places we call home are places of heartbreak, wherever we find ourselves in the world. But home is also a place where the heart can mend, and my heart needed to mend in Edmonton.

When I arrived in Edmonton after my time in Palestine, I had little money left and knew I would have to get a job soon. I found work as a security guard and that tided me over for four months until I got work as a systems analyst at the Capital Health Authority. The year following my return to Canada was filled with momentous world events, but the standout event was undoubtedly the bombing of the Twin Towers on September 11, 2001. I was staying at Uncle Faisal and Aunt Khadija's house at the time, and my aunt woke me up to come and see the events unfold. I could not believe it. I felt sick to my stomach. I went to work, where everyone was talking about it and watching TV in the corridors of the Royal Alexandra Hospital. My mind was racing. I heard a Muslim brother say, "Why did it have to be Muslims? This will kill us."

My colleagues who were not Muslim were horrified at the thought of everyone who had died, and of those who would die. For marginalized communities who are accustomed to collective punishment, the terrifying pause between hearing about a violent crime and waiting for media reports about the profile of the suspected attackers is like holding your breath underwater. When the answer comes that Muslims were responsible, we know these events will be used to justify sweeping *Patriot Acts*, Security Certificates, imprisonment without charges, violence against women in our communities, bullying of our youth and children, and renewed invasions on false pretenses. It is like coming up for air and taking a full breath of tear gas. Memories of the First Gulf War, which happened while I was a kid, came flooding back, and I could only expect that it would be worse this time.

But the Edmonton I returned to was a different city to the one I grew up in. While the Muslim voices had often stayed silent when I was a youth, the city had become a place where dialogue was more accepted, and more common. Jewish and Muslim leaders created news releases together, condemning the attacks, offering sympathy to the victims, and vowing to work together. As well, the members of the Edmonton Council of Muslim Communities, who had often been at odds with each other, pledged to work together.

At a time when suspicion was growing towards anyone in a hijab or prayer cap or who had darker skin, we found that in Edmonton people were coming to the Al-Rashid Mosque bearing flowers and cards, even though they were not Muslim. One man hugged the imam, saying, "We know you are part of this community. You're not like those terrorists."

As I grew tired of the monotony of systems analysis work, I sent my application to the University of Victoria for a PhD program in health informatics. Four months later, I got my response: I had been accepted into the program. I now had a plan to get my career on track, and I wanted a companion who would share with me the experience of connecting to my culture as a parent, passing on our ways to a next generation. With my acceptance to the University of Victoria in hand, I set out for the Garden City, known as the saying goes for its two main age groups: the newly wed, and the nearly dead. I hoped to become one of the former.

19

At First Sight

In 2003, I was in the second year of my PhD program and the end was in sight. It was time to think about settling down and finding a partner, but I wanted do things traditionally. I was never good with romance as a youth in Edmonton and knew I could not do it on my own. I needed help, which you often get too much of from an Arab Muslim family.

I took Uncle Yazan's advice to find a bride in the ancestral homeland and booked flights for my mother and me to Amman, Jordan. My mother, Hanan, or Umm Mowafa (mother of Mowafa) as she was known to family in Jordan, had grown up in Syria. Like my father's family, her parents had been displaced from Palestine. She was happy to help choose a bride for her son, and eager to begin planning a wedding. My aunt Sana knew many people, so we asked her to connect us with appropriate families in her area.

After we arrived in Jordan, Aunt Sana gave my mom the phone numbers of families with a daughter ready for marriage, and we began the process of finding me a bride. My mom would phone, say hello, talk about her eligible son, and request a visit. If the response was positive, we would go to meet the family at their home. I met women whom I sensed would not be happy if they were married to me; some who were beautiful but who did not feel comfortable with me; some whom I did not find attractive; and some who were not from a good family. I had an idea of who I was hoping would respond positively to our approaches, but she did not respond as I had hoped, and I gave up after several weeks of visits. I was exhausted and beginning to feel cynical.

Waking up one night, I prayed and wholeheartedly asked God to help me find my soulmate. A few days later, my aunt phoned, bubbling with excitement. "For years, we have known this family," she said, "and for the first time in eighteen years, their daughter came to my salon to get her hair done! She is pretty and religious." I had never seen my mom make a phone call so fast.

We were invited to come over at seven, when the father would be home. In North America, a young man might be a little nervous about meeting a girlfriend's father, but in Eastern culture, you are marrying an entire family, so the anxiety induced by a first meeting is multiplied many times over.

Dua's father was an engineer with a great reputation in Jordan. Dua herself was studying social work. The family members were elegant, the brothers and sisters were close. With my own family so scattered, I felt drawn to this family that displayed such a deep sense of togetherness. The house was tidy and spotless, something I knew my mother had noticed, for I could see her looking without seeming to. So far, it all looked promising.

Then my future mother-in-law said, "We don't care about money or anything like that. It is about who you are and your morals."

My future father-in-law asked two questions.

"Do you pray?"

"Yes," I answered.

"Do you smoke?"

"No."

These two questions seem simple, but they touch on foundational connections to God, health, and dealing with stress—something that I, as a nervous young man on the edge of getting married, would only begin to understand much later.

Aunt Sana had known Dua's family for years, and the initial interview had gone well, so the family agreed to let me meet Dua, especially since I would be returning to Canada shortly. My aunt, my mother, and their brother, Uncle Hisham, went with me to their house. When Dua walked in, wearing her hijab and abaya, the earth stopped. I knew that she was the woman I had asked God to help me find just the night before!

In my nervousness, the first question I asked her was "Do you know how to cook and clean?"

She laughed and said, "Are you looking for a maid or a wife?"

I blushed, not knowing how to react or act, but somehow we stumbled through our first encounter with each other. I was relieved that I could feel that she, too, was as interested in me as I was in her. I felt happy as we left, feeling that my prayers had been answered. My mother was also delighted and satisfied that she had helped the meeting go well.

My future father-in-law told me to visit any time. "Come here every day, if you like, to see my daughter, for as long as you want . . . come every single day!" So I did.

Eventually, Uncle Hisham, took me aside. "What are you doing, going every day?"

"But he invited me to . . ."

My uncle informed me that my future father-in-law's invitation had meant "Visit, perhaps, every couple of days." I was still learning how to interpret this Eastern-style generosity, and I have been confused by this many times since.

As the two families connected through the lengthy process of marriage, I got to know my own extended family better. The entire Househ family in Amman, a few dozen of us, arrived at the engagement ceremony in a very traditional way. My eldest uncle, Darwish, may God rest his soul, arrived in his keffiyeh and *bisht* (a flowing, outer cloak). He led the procession, with everyone else following behind him. We were about twenty to twenty-five men, sitting separately from the women.

Then a member of Parliament, Azzam Alhunaidy, who was a friend of my father-in-law and of Uncle Darwish, arrived, and everyone's faces beamed with pride. The elders spoke together for a bit; then my uncle addressed all who were gathered: "In the name of God, the gracious and most merciful ... and peace and blessing be on the Prophet Muḥammad. We are the Househ family from Palestine, the city of Lydda, and have come to your Alburini household to have our son Mowafa ask for the marriage of your daughter, Dua. Our son comes from a good family, and his father could not be here, so I am here in his place. My nephew is a good boy, doing his doctorate. He is educated, and he prays. I know this because we prayed together at the masjid last night. We come here to ask for your daughter's hand. What does your family say?"

Although the imam talks to the chosen woman to ensure that she is not being coerced into marriage, the acceptance of the wedding proposal is made by the bride's father or her eldest living male relative. My future father-in-law drew a long breath.

"In the name of God the most gracious most merciful ... peace and blessings be on the Prophet Muḥammad. First, we are honoured to have you and our guests in our home tonight, and we are honoured for the Alburini family and the Househ family to be connected. It is our honour to give our daughter to your son Mowafa. Please drink the coffee."

If he had said, "Don't drink the coffee," it meant that the family had not accepted the proposal. I didn't think I would hear those words, but something in me feared hearing them.

Uncle Darwish said to me, "Go kiss your father-in-law's hand." I stared at him, shocked. *Are you kidding?* I thought. It was an old tradition that generally isn't done anymore, but I could not embarrass my uncle by saying no, for it was a sign of respect, and if he said I had to do it, then I had no choice in the matter. After all, I was the one who had wanted to have a traditional arranged marriage. When the obligatory customs had been completed, the sheikh who was to perform the wedding ceremony stepped forward and did his part. Afterward, we signed the marriage contract and read the Fatiha, the first chapter of the Qur'an. The women started to make *zaghareet*, a high-pitched, celebratory ululation. There were drinks and *kanafa*, a traditional Palestinian cheese-pastry dessert soaked in syrup. After many good wishes and blessings, we all went home. I was full of food and coffee, but I floated the whole way home.

Although we were now married on paper, this initial engagement ceremony was only a first step that opened the door for us to get to know each other. We could not actually have the legal wedding until Dua's sponsorship paperwork was finished a year and a half later. This also gave me some time to get to know the culture I was marrying into better. It was my family's culture too, of course, but we were North Americans as well, and there were many differences that had arisen over the years. The Alberta-raised Househs were outgoing and direct to a fault, and I needed to adapt to the communication styles of my new family's culture, which included seeking consensus in a circular way. It can be tiring and confusing, and it was a stretch for me to see the logic of non-confrontational styles that didn't make sense to me at first.

I had always been straight up and never avoided conflict, and this was part of why I had never been good with wooing women like my other friends were. Despite my shortcomings, I survived the process with the help of knowledgeable women like my mom and various relatives. For the year that we spent on opposite ends of the world, emails were the main method of communication between Dua and me. I was scared: I didn't want to make the same mistakes as my father had. I waited, usually alone, with Dua in my heart. I walked around Victoria imagining what it would be like to have a companion and hoping for the best start possible to a new chapter in my life. I never wanted to experience the pain of divorce, as my parents had. In December 2004, I got a message to go to Jordan. Her visa was ready.

I had no time and, as a student, no funds, to prepare for the wedding. I got on a plane with my mom and asked Dua to pick a place where we could host the ceremony and reception with her family in Jordan.

On the day of the wedding, my family gathered at Uncle Darwish's home in Amman. We went to pick up my wife from her home, a sign of respect. When she came down, some members of her family were happy, and others were crying because they were saddened by the thought of Dua leaving her parents' home. My heart was racing. I felt overwhelmed, unsure whether I had the ability to meet this new responsibility. Dua seemed so much more collected and aware of how to move through the events of the evening. I was terrified, feeling that we didn't really know each other beyond communicating by text over the past year.

My aunt Karam let me use her Mercedes-Benz to take my wife to the wedding. As we entered the wedding hall, there was an Egyptian *zaffa*, a noisy parade with fireworks. This was followed by a procession announcing the wedding, with "thrones" for the couple, who were considered king and queen for the day. Family by family, the guests approached us to offer their congratulations and presents to the newlyweds.

I danced with my wife in the ladies' section. Then I went to talk to the male guests, who were seated in another room, chatting. Then I returned to the ladies' section to cut the cake with my wife and dance some more. When my male relatives joined us on the dance floor, the women put their hijabs on, tucking their hair inside. After a long day and evening, my wife and I drove to our hotel. It was our first time alone as a married couple.

20

Putting Down New Roots

After our wedding, Dua and I left Amman to fly back Victoria, where I was still finishing my PhD. Dua began volunteering as a Qur'an teacher at the mosque, and we went to community pot-luck events. She was also taking English courses, and while this helped with her integration into a new town, the suspicious looks she received and the language barrier she encountered made it hard to feel comfortable. Gradually, we made our two-bedroom apartment on Gorge Road into a home, preparing a room for the child that was on the way. Soon, the baby book started to fill up with pictures of moments with Dana.

Parenthood inspired bittersweet reflection on the challen-ges my own parents had faced. The extremes of joy and fear that come with marriage and parenthood make everything import-ant, and my focus became fixed on a small group of people. My parents and the community in Edmonton had struggled to fulfill their dreams for their families, yet, like so many Indigenous fam-ilies in North America who have lost their land, the ghosts of the past haunted my father and divided us from each other. With the guidance of those who saw me struggle as a young man, my way of coping was to connect the past, present, and future through my family and faith. Victoria, BC was a haven where my future career started to take shape. My academic interests in engineering and business were clarifying with purpose—I wanted to pursue how using data could provide more efficient healthcare.

In 2006, I was at school, working on my dissertation when the phone rang at home. Dua answered. It was Bakheet al-Dossari, the chair of health informatics at a new university in Riyadh, Saudi Arabia. He was calling to recruit me for their university. After chatting about the department's recruiting effort, Dua told him she would pass on the message to me. When I got home, I called him. I explained that I was still finishing my degree and that I would consider the offer after I graduated. Dua was excited about the prospect of moving closer to her family in Jordan, but rather than immediately making this move back to the Middle East, we went in a different direction—to northern British Columbia.

Rather than go to Riyadh, I accepted a contract as a planning and research analyst for the Northern Health Authority, working in an office in downtown Prince George. I helped develop health information systems, and my understanding of the situation in Palestine deepened as I witnessed the suffering of the First Nations people around me. I was trying to enhance health care services by gathering and interpreting data, but the chronic and acute health problems in First Nations communities—like diabetes, addictions, and suicide—were issues that could not be adequately addressed by the Health Authority. The source of the pain was much deeper—in the loss of land and family.

For Dua, these moves, first from Amman to Victoria, a small university city on Vancouver Island, and then to a very remote rural community in Prince George, came with major challenges. Dua was following a path similar to that of my parents, who had been among the first in our family to arrive in North America.

As we approached Prince George for the first time, we could see and smell the pulp mill in the town that would become our home.

The past, present, and future of the land on which Prince George is situated is connected to the Lheidli T'enneh First Nation, and many people from the surrounding nations live in this northern city. We soon learned about the many Indigenous women who had been murdered or gone missing along Highway 16 between Prince George and Prince Rupert, and that this stretch of road had become known as the Highway of Tears. Our hearts emptied—how sad that there was such extreme suffering here and in other parts of the world. I was just beginning to understand the depths of care and responsibility of family life. Dua, as a new immigrant, saw these connections more clearly than I did, and it was her concern for people and the suffering she saw that gave her a reason to stay and complete her studies in social work. As my work exposed me to the realities of health and life in northern communities, it became clear to me that Arab refugees are not the only people who have faced forced displacement from traditional lands and intentional settler policies of trying to decrease life chances in emerging generations. Dua and Dana were the centre of my life, and we were determined to make a home in this Western world.

One weekend in 2007, to expand Dua's experiences of Canadian culture, we decided to check out Barkerville, a "historical" tourist village that is, according to the promotional website, the "largest living-history museum in western North America." Going to this simulated frontier town, which celebrates settlers, felt surreal. I couldn't help but think of Canada Park, an Israeli national park that contains the ruins of three Palestinian villages destroyed by Israel in 1967 and that is funded by the Canadian Jewish community. As Dua waited in line at a vendor, she noticed a stranger staring at her hijab. He said, "I guess not much has changed over the centuries." Why, in public places where families go to enjoy fresh air, on the bus, or in the streets, is there a creeping entitlement to single her out and to mock her choices? As the remoteness of this northern region started to weigh on us, we began to plan our relocation closer to the traditional land of our people.

We moved to Saudi Arabia in 2009, and we now live in the Middle East like our parents did. I work at the University for Health Sciences in Riyadh, which was established in 2005. My family in Canada is concerned about us living in the shifting political sands of the Middle East, but the conditions in Saudi Arabia and Palestine are like night and day.

After visiting Palestine and now working in Saudi with many other Palestinians closer to my father's age, I am beginning to understand why my dad did not talk more about his difficulties and struggles. At times, he was enthusiastic about his memories, his face coming alive, his dark eyes bright. He is one of the few living Palestinian refugees who were born and lived in Palestine as it was in 1948. In my curiosity and need for connection, I try to drag information out of him. At times, I feel more like an interrogator than a son trying to discover his own past. I am not always sure of what my dad thinks about me raising a family in the Middle East. He is proud of what I have achieved, but every so often, he asks me questions that reveal his struggle to understand the new world he finds himself in.

"Tell me again . . . what is health informatics?" he will ask. "What do I tell my family and friends that you do? I really don't understand it."

My father may not have understood my reasons for moving to Saudi Arabia, but I had spent so little time in the Arab world, and I had such a strong desire to connect with the cultures and lands of my Arabic family. Dua and I had grown up in different environments, and I wanted to close the culture gap between us. In Riyadh, Dua was closer to her family and found herself in an environment she could relate to with greater ease. Moving to the Middle East was the right choice for me, Dua, and our children.

Living in Saudi Arabia helped me understand Arabic culture. I developed immense respect for the Saudi people. They taught me to be closer to my parents and to my wife. People were friendly and treated me with respect, which had not always been my experience up to that point in my life. We named our youngest daughter Loujain, which means "silver water" in Arabic. Loujain is our third child, and in 2017 we were blessed with a son, who we named Said after my father, as tradition requires. As parents, we try hard to bridge the gap between world our parents grew up in and the world our children will inherit. Time will tell how successful we have been.

I did not understand how North American I was until we started sharing a home in the Arabian Gulf. Moving to the Middle East in 2009 helped me understand Dua better, how she thinks, and how her Palestinian Arab identity that is connected to Jordan feels more grounded than my family, who ended up so far away in Alberta. As we criss-cross the ocean from Canada to the Arab Muslim world and back, we survive in places where we half-belong. Dua and our children have been changing locations, caught between push and pull forces; like my parents moving their children back to Jordan in 1985.

We have been trying to fit into an old new place, and not for the first time moving constantly, living with terrifying uncertainty and shouldering the burdens of uprooted children and lost ancestry. Dua and I pray this will work to the advantage of our children—they can already read both Arabic, right to left, and

English, left to right. Like many other families here, Dua and I plan to benefit from our time in the Gulf and eventually, her family and community in Jordan.

Now when I return to Canada, I go as Dr. Mowafa Househ, presenting papers at conferences about health care and technology. In my research, I focus on the use of Artificial Intelligence, social media, and mobile technology to promote patient care, improve health literacy, and with a more recent focus on mental health. Health informatics is a combination of information/computer science and health care, health medicine, and biomedicine. It covers everything from clinical guidelines and medical technologies to communication systems. In one project, I explored Islamic e-health, showing that it focuses primarily on spiritual health. To complement this existing trend, I investigated health information systems used during the Hajj to monitor the blood-glucose levels of Muslim patients fasting during the month of Ramadan. Seeing the life chances of all my relations severely harmed by displacement and hostility, has motivated my interested in digital health innovation that can scale solutions in a way that leaves no one on the margins. No one left behind.

The sharing of perfume samples in the refugee camp in Jordan, the arrangements my uncle required to seek treatment outside of Palestine, the attention to my injured eye in Edmonton, the kindness of strangers shown to my mother, and the care provided for my growing family as we patched together our wellbeing across regions—these moments and many others shared in this memoir are behind my drive to survive and address the harm of illness as well as the injustice of this intergenerational international catastrophe.

My father tries to express the impact of the Israeli-Palestinian conflict and the violence on his life. He says "I did not grow up in a religious place. I grew up in a refugee camp." Meanwhile, my independent mother has raised five children to value the peace that can be found in Islam to heal these wounds. Witnessing life under occupation in Palestine burned this need to heal into my mind, just as the grief and fear I felt standing outside our vandalized mosque as a teen in Edmonton remains in my heart.

Half-Belonging
in the World

In 2012, I visited Toronto with my mother. We had dinner at the same elegant hotel where we had been treated so kindly more than two decades earlier, when she had moved us across the country in distress. I don't think she remembered the place, but I did. I did not want to remind her, so I simply watched her enjoy the ambience of the hotel restaurant. We had a beautiful meal and enjoyed our time together, laughing about family stories and crying as we shared stories of our difficult past. As I continue to face the effects of occupation and displacement in my family, I need to share the complexity of my individual and our collective experiences as Palestinians.

From Edmonton to Hebron, every Palestinian I meet is affected in some way by the occupation. I saw this during my time as a young returnee in Palestine, and I have seen it more recently while working as an instructor in the Gulf. Meeting Palestinians, other Arabs, exposes me to the spectrum of care and dignity in Arab cultures. My parents struggled to repair, reclaim, and represent this, both before and after being displaced to Canada. The relative stability of a Palestinian family in the diaspora changes people's lives but not their collective memory. Passports are granted, temporary shelter is offered, and reunions are made possible. As Palestinians in exile, away from the occupied territories, we sit together, share food, and pray for our families in the diaspora and the homeland. We pray that our efforts will secure our territory and sustain our culture for future generations. Home and land are inseparable in our psyches and hearts. In a different region, like Jordan, Canada, or Syria, a tent, a concrete shelter, or a house might feel familiar, or even comfortable, yet we inherit this fragmentation like cuttings from uprooted saplings. Until we return to the original soil that has nourished our ancestors, we wait and struggle in the long shadow of the Nakba tree.

ACKNOWLEDGEMENTS

I would like to thank my mentor, Elder Brother and Uncle Yazan Haymour, the Arab Prince of Edmonton. He was the one who initially encouraged me to finish this important work and who supported me throughout its writing. I am also grateful to my good friend Simon Moll, who spent many nights reviewing specific sections and providing me with feedback. I would like to extend my deepest thanks to Peter Midgley and to the serendipity that brought us together. His insights, challenges, and recommendations have ultimately produced a richer and more compelling narrative that will, I hope, contribute to a much larger commentary on the Palestinian Nakba. Last, I owe a special thanks to Pamela Holway, at Athabasca University Press, who believed in this project and gave me the opportunity to share it with the world.